BY PETER DAVISON

POEMS

AUTOBIOGRAPHY

EDITOR

PRAYING WRONG

PRAYING WRONG

NEW AND SELECTED POEMS
1957–1984

PETER DAVISON

ATHENEUM   *New York*

1984

Thanks to the editors of the following publications for their hospitality to the new poems in this book. Some appeared in earlier versions.

AMERICAN SCHOLAR: *The Vanishing Point*
THE ATLANTIC: *Stern Stuff, The Everlasting, Crossing the Void, Last Infirmity*
LITERATURE AND BELIEF: *Absalom, The Housewife's Paradise*
LITTLE BALKANS REVIEW: *Impossible People*
NEW ENGLAND REVIEW AND BREAD LOAF QUARTERLY: *Questions of Swimming, 1935*
PLOUGHSHARES: *Low Lands*
POETRY: *The Money Cry, Monosyllables [Not a Dilemma], Moving into Memory, Remembering Eurydice, The Revenant*
TENDRIL: *Night Watch*

Poems from the following previously published books are included in this volume:

THE BREAKING OF THE DAY, copyright © 1958, 1959, 1960, 1961, 1963, 1964 by Peter Davison; published by Yale University Press

THE CITY AND THE ISLAND, copyright © 1964, 1965, 1966 by Peter Davison; published by Atheneum

PRETENDING TO BE ASLEEP, copyright © 1967, 1968, 1969, 1970 by Peter Davison; published by Atheneum

WALKING THE BOUNDARIES, POEMS *1957–1974*, copyright © 1974 by Peter Davison; published by Atheneum

A VOICE IN THE MOUNTAIN, copyright © 1975, 1976, 1977 by Peter Davison; published by Atheneum

BARN FEVER AND OTHER POEMS, copyright © 1978, 1979, 1980, 1981 by Peter Davison; published by Atheneum

TO THE MEMORY OF
JANE TRUSLOW DAVISON
AND FOR OUR CHILDREN
ANGUS AND LESLEY

AUTHOR'S NOTE

Nearly all poems utter a prayer, whether explicit or not, a plea for some sort of consequence, even if it's no more than a call for order or a complaint to the management. Who is to tell us whether prayers, even if we get them right, may be heard, or by whom, or how answered? We pray as carefully as we can.

The passage of time has prompted me to tune up—when I could do so without second-guessing—some of the poems that have continued to mean most to me, especially if the words in which they presented themselves turned out to be more dunderheaded than I could continue to tolerate. So I have in this volume now and then attempted (as, for example, in "Haskell's Mill") retroactive revision. I pray that the results will register somewhere.

Since I began practising this intractable craft, I have benefited from the generous advice and support of a number of fellow poets, to some of whom earlier volumes were in fact dedicated. Edward Davison, Robert Frost, Alastair Reid, Dudley Fitts, William Abrahams, Esther S. Yntema, Mary Jo Salter, George Starbuck, and Linda Gregerson have all given much. Harry Ford has given even more. And, most recently, Joan Edelman Goody has given most.

PETER DAVISON
March, 1984

CONTENTS

THE VANISHING POINT (1984)

FROM BARN FEVER (1981)

FROM A VOICE IN THE MOUNTAIN *(1977)*

FROM WALKING THE BOUNDARIES *(1974)*

FROM THE BREAKING OF THE DAY AND OTHER POEMS *(1964)*

THE VANISHING POINT

(*1984*)

WINTERING OVER

Only spring sun, so tense, so pale,
so unestablished, could manage the matter,
but once again as every year
this weathered old beast
unfolds a plan to hurl
a filament of itself
across the arroyo
and build its annual bridge
between past and future.
If I stand back, keep
an eye on things, I may
witness my own delivery
from high above the female proscenium,
cave of fertility and its enactment.
This event is me. Do I know it?
Am I this very thing?
I answer my own questions.
An intimate galaxy of genes
reiterates the permanence of change,
and this great attic of language,
lovingly rummaged,
will welcome a fresh brood of tenants
into the most tumbledown of houses.

Let us live here.

THE VANISHING POINT

(New Year's Day 1984)

Snow crept up overnight as we slept
and powdered the surface of the earth so lightly
the footpaths stirred, as smooth as dusted skin.
An uncut beard of grass darkened the field.
I had awakened to the shimmering landscape
from a sleep sunk in sullen dreams, entombed
in the companionship of friends long dead
who accelerated along gravel country roads
or city streets crammed with traffic
toward no end anyone would have wanted to reach.
Their destination was a point deeper than ever
in the closed and unforgiving past
where love enacts its remorseless guzzling.

This morning, though, was dusted with the present
as though brushed by the smoky fragrance
of sleep. It held there for the moment.
No wind stirred up the snow along the branches,
no wheel crushed down a snowflake on the road.
This present moment, exquisitely poised,
had not yet given in to the scramble of time
but seemed to hold itself back from moving on
out of a night which hurtled in drunken zigzags
through one of the dreams where we are never alone.
Carried by trains, motorcycles, elevators,
we are always passengers, always companioned,
sniffing out the smelly trails of childhood,
flaunting a thousand newly-sewn disguises.
Where those dreams take us, no matter how eager
their search, they never end in arrival.

Now the present is inching toward the future.
At the silent feeding station chickadees chirp.
Over the marsh black air flourishes flecks
of irregular white, more snowflakes, *storme still.*
The sky as it unbends relents a little
and grows lighter. A dog barks in protest

at the iron day, indignant at its silence.
The perfection of this morning hour has yielded,
without anticipation, to the fact
that time is coasting forward, turning momentum
into the new year's elliptical glide.

Poised on the incoming day, between tides
of sleep and waking, I ride on the waters of time,
whose movement, steady as the orb of earth,
makes only one general statement: *Change is all.*
The weather system, the troubling dreams of travel,
a scrap of geography discarded here
in the glacial scree of leftover landscape—
these happenings seek no end, no destination.
Each moment wishes us to move farther on
into a sequence we can follow at most
to vanishing point. We can see no farther,
though time seems to pause and wait for us at times
and measure us and move along again.

THE HOUSEWIFE'S PARADISE

Across the scene dance dromedaries,
tigers, prancing horses, zebras,
"two and two of all flesh
wherein is the breath of life."
The sceptre tail of Lion commands
a procession of beasts under father trees.
The sky has clouded over. Waters gurgle
to tug the ark by its hull. Will Noah preserve
one pair of every sort of genital,
the periphrastic families of the earth?

In Pennsylvania preacher Edward Hicks,
fleeing from ghostly swords,
peered through the branches of a half-cut forest
and brushed in scenes of peaceful time-to-come
as promised in plain statements by the Lord.
A hatted Quaker smacked a friendly palm
against a feathered red man's on a beach.
Smiling Lion crouched to nibble hay
by the side of pussycat Ox.
Leaves did not tumble, wounds did not leak blood,
lambkins never crumpled in a colic.
Rooftops, safe against God's lightning,
kept rainspots off the pewter plates of housewives,
sheltering the honeyed entropies of peace.

On working farms the gravid ewes give
bloody birth on bare barn floors. The lambs
lie there, at first unblinking. Mothers lick
mucus from the nostrils and the eyes,
and offspring totter to suck at the flesh
that further heats their breath.
In May longlight, February lambs
may drop the teat and munch the sea of grass
as noisily as their great toothed sisters,
and then, why not, next fall, be mounted
by the greedy-shouldered ram
with gasps of satisfaction, breath of life?

6

In Hicks' landscapes horses won't gallop:
they prance, curvet, lie at rest.
Even George Washington's steed stands easy,
deaf to captains and the shouting.
The Peaceable Kingdom, shelter for Friends,
shelters them coolly under a cloudless roof
in a clearing as solid as a square stone house.

Here is the land of cider, laundry, bread,
the housewife's paradise, with love lavishly spread
in quilt or bright-scrubbed doorstep
to shed its inner light
and banish every howling of the spirit.
Cast it out elsewhere, anywhere you will,
and pit the blessed order of a kitchen shelf
against the barbarism of the kill.

IMPOSSIBLE PEOPLE

They stand very close to us, so close
they end up looking like our other selves:
parents to start with, then teachers,
then lovers, ("O thou, that I had never
laid eyes on thee, such a mistake!")
then characters straight out of the lives
(or works) of Dickens or Robert Lowell or other
impossible people. They are discovered mostly
as if by children spying on a party.

Impossibles turn up at every turn
until, as we lapse lazily into age,
they strike us as just a little less
impossible—or not impossible at all—
until the moment when—bang!—
the little old lady whips out a Siamese flag
from the rump of her knickers, or a tycoon
with metallic eyes, seated across the glistening
conference table, seizes my hand, and without
a word starts kissing my fingers.

Impossible teeters lushly, braving a freeway,
and snarls (obscenity) at every fucking car
whose passing wheels he nearly tumbles under.

Impossible gives me the hip in the checkout line.

Impossibles march gaily for Gay Pride,
ashaming any spectator a marcher would
yearn to be matey with, mincing

atinkle with bangles and lavender marcel
just like their mothers after the hairdresser.

Impossible employer gathers the staff together
and shyly rises to his speech, presenting
a gift to me, unwarned recipient.
He smiles. Unwrapped, it's lovely. It's a bronze-
and-green-morocco-bound *Prometheus Bound*!
I see him smile as I unwrap the wrappings
and murmur thank-hims for the ball-and-chain.

Impossible near-and-dears adopt disguises:
my college roommate swanning at our twenty-fifth,
an uncle whose cataracts outlived his wits,
my wife, unnoticed behind a vodka gimlet—
where did I lose track of all these strangers?

We bend the mind so hard in search of answers
that we forget, it's questions seeking answers
put marrow in the bone. No possible prayer,
taken alone, can teach us any cure
for the loss of face that follows loss of life.
So face it: if the fact of my existence—
to be, to rise, to lift the weight, to move—
seems on the face of it impossible,
e pur si muove, swore one impossible old
star-watcher. You see? The *other* one is moved!

QUESTIONS OF SWIMMING, 1935

(For Robert Penn Warren)

What was the nub of wonder? Was it
the man, giant to my child-eyes, strapping
a shiny black rubber bathing cap over the cap
of his red hair, plugging his nostrils and ears,
and lowering his lean body into the yellow
lake in Colorado, down into the frightening
water, to begin the steady trudgen
that took him, as long as my skipping patience
could endure, steadily farther from sight
as far as the far shore, a mile, and without
pause, brought him back to me, bobbing
far out in the water, then thrashing,
then finally splashing, and gasping and rising,
and then, again, human and near me, dripping and walking?

Wonder at the man, or at the task?
What sort of way was it to spend
an hour in thrashing straight across a lake
and, turning, swimming straight back to the start?
Where was he setting out for when he began, fresh?
Where had he been to when he returned, winded?

Or take the style: laboring akimbo,
a steady crawl across the sheet of water
without a pause to whoop or whistle or blow,
a style as awkward as inexorable,
in which the completion of the task seemed to count
more to the swimmer than not drowning.

The lake? A captive body
the dry climate had permitted
to rest between the knees
Boulder had bulldozed to keep

the water from evaporating: a reservoir.
The man swam back and forth between its walls.

What of the rhythm of the exercise?
Not like a dog or deer that simply walks
on water, but a dactyl, a quantitative
excursus, a distribution of forces between
the limbs, these legs working like scissors,
these arms working like flails, these lungs
working like bellows, this mind working,
working on lessened oxygen, this body
moving against every interference to imitate
its forgotten grandfather, the fish.

To the destructive element submit yourself,
and with the exertions of your hands and feet
make the deep, deep sea keep you up.
Once kept up, where do we go from there?
To the headwaters, the spawning ground?
To the floating pyre, the fire ship?
To the other shore? Which is the other shore?
Could it be the place where a boy could watch
a man pull on the helmet of a bathing cap
and set out, swimming, for a farther shore?

LOW LANDS

(For Jacob van Ruysdael and for John Updike)

This topsoil coverlet, dampened by a coast
that's warmed by mediation of the sea,
shall be transformed—I'll paint them!—into hills
erected by a netherlander's fancy,
crags bearing castles and churches, theologies
for which a million suffering soldiers died.

A birch tree, blasted, leans along one border
to balance the other, a dark insolent rainbow.
Between the two a castle falls to ruin.
Light burns inside the trunks of standing trees,
gleams in the rump of a carthorse going to water.
See how this goat hesitates, beside a ford,
whether to cross over to the side of the angels?
"Hunting a Stag": the doomed innocent quarry
plashes ill-suited hooves across a marsh,
unsparingly pursued by dogs, hunters,
and the light and shade from several hundred trees.
Above this scene hawks, vultures, owls and doves
read speeches from the drama of salvation.

I will distend the hummock's trickling water
by doubling the distance it can fall.
Infirm foundations lift my tottering spires.
Hills that my parish eyes have elevated
will bulge up higher, skyward, birdward, Godward,
belittling the cities of the plain,
the fishing fleets, plowed fields, hedged pastures
whose view gives no more length than the horizon.
From Italy I shall import a landscape
that some of us prefer to thoughts of heaven,
transforming lowlands into the lofty hills
which the Most High desired for His abode.

INTIMACIES

1. *Mates*

Stronger than vows or roses is the scent
that gathers from a sweet conjunction of lives,
as when two animals, nosing into love,
have snouted each other's parts and found them good.
Each such discovery discovers more,
roaming savannah, sousing in mire, snoring in caves.
When the mood strikes they strike out in different directions,
expecting to slouch to some waterhole at sunset
where, after dark, they will curl up together,
nose to tail, as easy as potatoes.

2. *He Loves Animals,*

all kinds of animals. Ducks, chickens, turkeys.
dogs, pigs, sheep. Just loves taking care.
If he forgets sometimes
to give them water, or if they
have a way of dying of the heat,
or malnutrition, or worse,
everything that happens to them comes
of his way of showing
how important it is for him
to show his love for them.

3. *Prints*

Hoofprints of a plowhorse!
who's trampled steelshod
from end to end of the flower bed,
filing in front of one stalk
of withered delphinium
but threading behind another
along the granite wall.
There the prints vanished.
Oh, how I glowered
at such brutal trespass!
And when I walked out
to steal a second look
even worse had taken place:
a filigree of fox tracks
printed primly inside
the massive dents of hoof,
passing by the wall,
sparing the flowers.

ABSALOM

King David's anguish bristled,
whimpered, cocked his head
like a lost hound
listening for its master.
The prince crazed into a muddle
of tears at every teaching.
Riddles sent him areel.

What of such a son, whose father
refuses to do him harm
but turns away his face?
Could he ever earn the right
to inherit the crown of Saul
until he felt emboldened,
like his father before him,
to put on the unthinkable colors
of the king's worst enemy?

This too sent him areel.
Why not, he must have thought,
get dressed in overalls
and gallop off on a mule
along the first track to the left?
This led him, as it happened,
in under a stunted
ruin of an oak,

and now he hangs there, helpless,
target for the average man,
doomed by the tendrils
of human hair
he couldn't help growing,

and the king, as helpless as he
in the chamber above the gate,
covers his face again:
Would God I had died for thee,
O Absalom, my son, my son!

CROSSING THE VOID

(for Stanley Kunitz)

I pick my crooked way
across a half-built bridge
past left-behind lunchpails,
rusting wrenches, cables
coiled scattershot
half across the span.
Could my scream be heard?
No, nor anyone catch
a glimpse of a body falling
to the rocks, hammered to pieces
by the brawling stream below.

I count my footsteps toward
the emptiness ahead
with no memory pushing me,
not the milk-scented kisses of childhood,
nor the prickle of revenge,
nor the black hounds of grief.
Against my face
droplets of flannel mist
dash tiny explosions.

Misguided by travel,
I know that without ground
I can hear no music, yet
unless I go on I'll be barred
from footing ashore
in rigging, on bridges,
clambering or crossing. As I approach
the vanishing point, I begin to feel
a half-remembered sickness
as when the waterfilled seaboot
pulls down, and then the list,
heave and plunge
of sinking planking.

THE MONEY CRY

My daughter cries when we have to talk about money.
"I can't help it," she wails. "I don't want to cry,
I just cry." How can a father blame her?
I set her straight by setting her allowance
or trying to mold the world to snug her budget
or preaching homilies about expense
and self-sufficiency. Foresight. *Foresight.*
All the while, quietly, helplessly, she cries.

Dollars of course can give a girl her head
with beads and shawls, or buy her sweet shampoos
and the acrid clangor of recorded music.
But dollars too could set her hands to work,
scrubbing pots and pans, mucking out stables.
No wonder money makes her cry! I can't
help wincing when I sit to pay the bills
from Progressive Oil or Dr. Leon Leach,
recalling the time it cost to raise the money,
and shiver when paychecks hiss across my blotter.
What will smear off? What is the handling charge?

I'd warn you to be wary of anyone
whose eyes light up at each percentage point
as though life were an electronic game
with nothing to describe it but the score.
The hunt's the game, not the computation,
yet all the while the world presents its bills,
and we sit paying them on Friday night
while everybody else is at the movies.
Listen! Don't cry. You get it and you spend it.
Take it and pass it on. That stuff won't kill you.

LAST INFIRMITY

O poem, poem! What possibility
has either of us got to be remembered
unless we can appeal over my head?
What if next Tuesday as I cross the street
that takes me to the cleaners I should walk
under the wheels of a truck (Calvucci & Sons/
Produce/ Revere Mass) while thinking of
a way to the right result in Nicaragua?
What would become of dear unfinished you,
crammed dogeared in a folder, vulnerable phrases
half-scratched-out? Whose hand then would smooth you,
uncrumple you, berate you? You and I
would have to take a powder together, ashes
in a tarnished urn, scraps of desperate paper
scuttling across the dump, your message whelmed
by the flurry of a thousand scavenger gulls.

NOTHING SUDDEN

1. *Monosyllables*

Here, says hot body,
stretched under pines
tossed by a westerly,
here, says skin.

Now, say sharp senses,
dizzied by mockingbirds
in the wisteria,
now, say ears.

This, say fingerpads,
dabbling along a plank
where the grain roughens,
this, says touch.

Wait, says the quick breath
at the first quiver
of a thigh stirring,
wait, says love.

See, says inquisitor,
flaying the pagan
ribcage from backbone,
that says *kill*.

I, says abandonment,
whispering hot words
to a cold pillow,
I, says husk.

Then? says memory,
then I was just a child,
then I loved tenderly.
Then, says echo.

Down, says the petal-fall.
Down, says the prophet.
Down down derry down
down, says drastic.

2.   *Night Watch*

Behind the sooty hill a violet sky
turns purple as the earth vanishes.
House-finches, nuthatches drop their suet
to wing for the woods.
The last of the daytime gulls has flapped away
to outer, colder islands.
In the who-hours an owl, downpasture,
breathes its wicked song from the pear-tree.

Tomorrow, many wakeful hours away,
when the sun singles out the feeding station,
faded goldfinch, chickadee, grosbeak and titmouse
will already have come from the woods.
The night-warmed dog will be whimpering
once again for the truth of open air.
Gravid sheep, restless, cramped
after their huge night in the black barn,
will be crowding the gate of their pen,
edging one another aside
to make a break when the gate swings.

What else is there to expect?
Things, beasts, want out, want in.
Behind those curtains can she still be sleeping?

3.   *Moving into Memory*

As long as those last words are never spoken
we can touch each other lightly
and sit here side by side
in the descending sun.
Our hands often creep
into one another's palms:
every other form of seeking
has gone lame or dry.
O dark sunbeam, my bed light, my cheer,
brightener of houses, freshener of shade,
the only gift I can be sure to keep
is this reaching and touching.
You will be allowed to keep nothing.

I keep unsure memory, and none.
The piano, glittering under delectable mountains,
has lost its way to the center of the music.
Silence gapes to swallow
the provocations of your laughter.
Though our days together are few,
the thunder of syllables
fills a black valley with light
while the wind whistles its own song
from the faraway edge of the glacier.

4.   *Stern Stuff*

The ashes, done up in stiff white paper
with hospital folds sealed over at each end,
lie dizzily beside the hole we've dug.
Tan talcum silt, powdered by two years' drought,
sifts out of a shovel. We watch the canister
tumble into the hole and lie alone.
Those ashes, while they held their lively form,
glowed flowery with every kind of laughter
and drove an ingenuity of will
to keep her vivid in a fading world.

Is this how we choke, in cataracts of dust?
What stern stuff it is, crumpling
the twigs of brittle, lace-veined wings
and chafing the light from smoky diamond eyes.

5.   *Remembering Eurydice*

I have lost the best of women.
Once again water irrigates
the scars, the gravel.
It was nothing sudden:
death set a stamp on her body
but not on her laughter.
We cowered together like children
at a flash of lightning,
imagining whether it would strike,
learning the tune of truth.

In a meadow peppered with daisies
she hung a screened tent
where she could be shaded
to tell the hours of summer,
gazing across pastures
where sheep grazed, paused
to wonder at the woman
seated, sorrowing.
Only her dog, mutely
privy to her loss of stance,
watched her tidy up her life's house
alone. When friends came
she smiled to keep them from grieving.

Now we can barely remember,
while woods and grasses
which remember nothing
offer us all we have to keep
but the stone that cries her name.

6. *The Everlasting*

A fist of flowers, anonymous as prayers,
a dozen field-plucked purple asters, droop
prone on a ledge a yard below that name
chased deep into harsh rock. Only four letters,
forty-nine years dismembered by a dash, peep pink
from the thorax of the granite ledge she loved.
Some florist roses fill a water glass
leaning atilt beneath the ledge's foot.
I can guess at the names of those who gathered flowers
or forked a couple of bills across a counter,
but, as the petals wilt below a name
that will outlast all eyes that read it now,
they speak as well as names or voices can
about fragility, flowering, fading away:
they speak for frost and death. The asters speak
out of a world of change, of repetition,
for those events that only happen once.

7. *The Revenant*

Last night, rummaging for scissors
in a back drawer, his fingers touched
something alive, not alive,
a pouch concealed under papers,
an envelope with no address.
In it, a lock of graying hair,
lopped from her head before the Cytoxin, cure-all,
not able to save her,
had struck her bald.
His hand now cradled one part
that had sprouted from her body,
many times assenting to
the touch of his fingers.
Her hair! The only frailty
she'd admit to! Her doctor,
never lowering his gaze,
told her she had a year to go,

adding of course he could "make her
more comfortable" with chemotherapy.
Her hands flew to her head, frightened birds
to save her hair. They fell at once
fluttering to her lap. She had to laugh
at herself, the hands. But not at the hair.
"I'm sorry," she said, aghast
at her own reasons.

FROM

BARN FEVER AND OTHER POEMS
(*1981*)

GIFT: The act, right, or power of giving.   *Webster*

Some quality or endowment given to man by
God or a deity.   *Webster*

With respect to real estate, formerly, any
form of alienation.   *Webster*

Something given to corrupt. A bribe.
Oxford

(German) Poison, toxin, virus, venom;
virulence, malice, fury.   *Cassell's German
Dictionary*

(Swedish)   Marriage

A gift in anticipation of impending death
is revocable until the death of the
giver, and then becomes absolute.   *Webster*

FOR JANE, WRITING

For over twenty years you have endowed me
with poems it seemed to me I had discovered
and with nearly every stability
I knew enough to know.
Your laughter freckles the horizon,
aurora meridionalis.
You sit in a work chair
the way a heron stands—
motionless, gazing down at the paper.
Then, with the flicker of a smile,
you lean for the fish
with pencil or stammering key.

SLEEPING BEAUTY VARIATIONS

(for Peter Shaffer)

Marriage or poison. Which was the gift
   that struck princes limp at the castle wall
like stones become too heavy to lift?

Matchmaker smirked, courtiers sniffed,
   godmother grinned from the head of the hall.
Marriage or poison, which was the gift?

Supple Aurora, maiden adrift,
   sheds blood, turns woman and takes the fall,
stone become too heavy to lift.

The world knows ways to give short shrift
   to sex that smothers itself in a pall
of marriage or poison. Which *was* the gift?

Upstairs the sleepers stir and shift.
   Time trickles down to bury us all,
stones become too heavy to lift.

The race we know is not to the swift.
   Slow sleeps out his life in a stall.
   Marriage or poison, which was the gift?
The stone become too heavy to lift?

JANUARY 1977

You had "never been absent." The nation hissed
  with blizzards. Telephone rang:
your voice from Tulsa. My heart and tongue
  interfered to say no more than
    "I miss you,"

blotting out news of white skies that had frozen
  sheep dead where they stood,
news of the illness of children. My love
  for your body skated across
a continent chilled to its heart with low temperatures
    setting new records.

Your voice had faded. Dreams reinforced
  the remoteness: I'm shut from our house,
from your bed, kneeling bareshins in slush.
  Dream islands breed
poisoned shellfish, dream bridges
  won't reach. My hands
tingled to cup your breast but shut
    as cold as the plains.

ON ITHACA

Settling at home, after Calypso, Circe
and Nausicaa, in Penelope's olive-tree bed,
among flocks of sheep and swine, surrounded by orchards,
how will Odysseus die? Will Penelope fuck him to death?
Or will he take to drinking with the swineherds?
In a pool Odysseus regards his body, comely
as when the women bathed it, and Athene
touched it with ambrosia till it glowed.
Later, abed, he dreams of Polyphemus,
the red-hot stake, the shriek, the sizzling eyeball,
that other flock of sheep, the great ram for escape,
the suitors feasting in the high-roofed hall,
the gouts of blood that spurted from his arrows.

WORDLESS WINTER

1. *Clinical Depression*

who cares what name you call it   here it comes
curling around the house in the dark like mist
that has no dampness   settling on my chest
like a weightless bird   tell it to go away
shout   clap your hands   let them stare
this visitor has no parents   where it lives
when it isnt invading innocent islands
I cannot guess for the life of me   I guess
it must have habitation in my cells
imprisoned like a foaming lunatic   shaking
the bars of my body   keeping the entire penitentiary
awake   baying me moonward night after night

who has seen low pressure   neither you nor I
but to deny the fact of my possession by it
is to declare myself swept clean of devils
and weep   goodbye depression   hello anxiety

2. *The Clinic*

When you say, "You haven't
done anything wrong," you must mean
that if I had done it, it could not be wrong,
being my act.

Such high regard the doctor
professes for the patient! That my most
ravenous desire should be characterized
as innocently as a pail of milk,
or one leg thrown dreamily over another!

Could you have meant that all sins
are equal, that there's "nothing
abnormal" in such behavior?

Then fact steps up with more
than moral news: *We found
cancer cells on the slide.*

You declare, "You haven't done
anything wrong." And I reply,
    "Haven't I?"

3.   *Willing Her to Live*

O, she's dying all right. But maybe
no faster than anyone else,
as Mark Twain said in response
to certain inquiries.
Among the remnants of a harvest,
sweating and staring in my garden,
I shovel dark infusions of manure
across pale autumn soil
in layers of enriching history,
stuff that cattle had devoured,
chewed over, passed through
before keeping a date with the butcher.

As I excite topsoil for next year
I wonder who will eat what's not yet grown
or whether anyone will plant it.
Wetly, blindly I keep shovelling.
Earth snatches compost back
like a transfusion and will not pause
to keep a leaf attached
in response to prayers or tears
or the use of shovels.

4.   *Frozen Drought*

Surprising sunshine has ruled more than a hundred days
this bare winter. Snow has forgotten itself.
The ground lies hard as stone and flat with dust

as though the surface were peeling in the wind
and blowing off to hell or to dust-heaven.
Neighbors and newspapers speak of the oddity,
snowless New England! Week after week blows by
and the ground grows dryer and the teeth grit.
The nose seals up against an invasion
of drought in Eastern air that never tasted
the brown dark of the dust over bleeding Kansas.

5. *Householder*

What can explain this ebb-tide of emotion,
this failure of joints and parts,
this position, as intolerable as
a turned turtle?
Hand will not clench on its pen,
head mislays its calling.
Heart? Content to keep beating.

This unfever has its blessings:
the bleaching out of anger.
A sensibility confined
to the predictable.
Indoor plants, domesticated animals.
No wild birds, no wild weather.
An implacable appetite
for things as they are. A nice gratitude
for the unresisted passage of time.

As householder I have felt
entitled to hope for better.
Now I pray to keep out of bed,
ask for no worse.
My friends hear nothing from me
once highly regarded, nor
do my enemies.
I have been taught by mixed blessings,
poisoned apples,
to sit apart, muscles clenched like marble.

6. *Stalemate*

Her will has worked
to the surface,
outcarving that smooth
genetic chisel that incised
rills running like inlets
toward her cornflower-blue eyes.
I kiss their corners.

Whatever it is that keeps
her harnessed
to the burden of her body
has impressed a set
of stretch marks on the forehead—
reinforcements.

Her face, a landscape, carries
the colors of contending armies:
a tug of joy, eyes lit with laughter;
a nagging hermit mask;
a cloud of pain.

7. *After Winter Slaughtering*

Our pigs have spent weeks away from their pen,
but hoofprints frozen in midnight mud
remember in ice the shape of a thigh
that, slaughtered, severed, relieved of blood,
lies cold in the dark as a blinded eye
counting lineup shots of arrested men.

8.   *The Writing Lesson*

Miss Daisy M. Johnston enforced her rules:
no wiggling, talking, or gum.
Hands clasped, or flat on the desk,
never out of sight in the lap.
Miss Daisy gospelled the Palmer Method:
write, write, write with the arm, not with the fingers;
push and pull as though conducting music.
The pencil must be held airily, unsqueezed,
guided through wrist, thumb, and elbow,
mastered by the shoulder,
guided by the waist.

Who, learning letters in this fashion,
could reserve adequate breath
to shriek for help
when muscles clenched in complaint
and the center of the body disclaimed them
and the poet, hands flat on the desk,
no wiggling, talking, or gum,
felt the dark cadence castigate his arm?

MY LADY THE LAKE

It is the lake within the lake that drowns.
Sunbeams gnaw into its dark, never again
to be released as light. The lake swallows
whatever it is fed. It eats its ice each spring,
nibbles for years at fallen twigs and timber,
engorges the heat of summer with each sunset,
closes around corpse of dragonfly and beaver.
By its waters I have sat down and wept, without
taking any comfort or return
except for the offer of what it has translated:
frogs, crayfish, sticklebacks. The trout
stocked by a prescient owner crammed themselves,
after the passage of several seasons, up
against its banks to die. It devoured their bones.
Still water gives us only a reflection.
Whatever we cast in, it will accept,
and in such lakes within the lake we drown.

THE RAM BENEATH THE BARN

Deep in the dark beneath foundation walls
the thick ram lies, his bent forefeet tucked under.

The droppings of a winter foul his straw,
but I dare no longer venture to his level
with grain, hay, water. I lower them to him
as to a tribe closed off by mountain snows.

He walks out into the sun, looks up at me,
his eyes expressionless as agates. He waits
for the moment of revenge. One day he may
catch me in a corner! Meanwhile, to prime his aim,
he taps his head and horns against the granite.

Of course when autumn comes he will again
curl up his lips into the sneer of lust
and leap his docile ewes, rolling their stupid
eyes as he does them his service—

but in this March we stare each other down,
two rams caught in a thicket by the horns.

INTERVAL

In the thick air of early September
mornings, crows call uninterrupted,
no competition. The whirr of katydids
keeps up an incessant thermograph
of sound, invisible orchestra
rising with light and heat,
falling with cold and dark
to steal the place of songbirds in the spectrum.

In the trees squirrels scramble
to stuff their pouches
with a season of beech nuts.
In the garden they shinny
up sunflower stalks to keep
the black seeds from falling prey
to incoming winter birds.
Tomatoes enrich their sagging vines
like Christmas baubles.

Except for one abandoned chick
too slow or small to fly, lying broken
and dead beside the lawnmower,
the barn has emptied of swallows.

New piglets, just learning
the taste of man's food, skitter
away from the fence each time
a wagging dog approaches.
Geese roost in the shade.
Sheep munch stolidly whatever
green blades survive
as members of the yellow medley of grass.

On such days between
their summer jobs and school
the children sleep till noon,
clothes and towels swathing
the floor like serpents.

In the meadow a girl exercises
a long-barreled grey gelding
with patches on his rump
and a tail like a chieftain's whisk.
They canter together around and around the field.
Katydids lower their buzz.

Black leaves are scarcely moving
on the trees. Along the wires
and in the willow branches
a thousand tree swallows stir and twitter,
awaiting a signal
to set off for Yucatán.

LAMBKILL

(Sheep Laurel, kalmia angustifolia)

Yielding far more than we had ever sown—
lushness of fescue laced with grapevine
and poison ivy, raspberries loud with bees—
the land flowed with milkweed and honeysuckle
in surpluses that seemed to call for forage
by expansionist sheep. They had already munched
three pastures down to rugs. We felled and set
five dozen posts, strung a furlong of wire,
and set up gates to keep the sheep shut in.

At first they didn't like this newest pasture,
something about the wind, the angle of the sun,
marsh flies buzzing around their flipflop ears.
They slept burrowing their muzzles under each other.
Waking, they browsed their way through the inscrutable,
bawling out their wish for a view of level grass,
hungry for simplicity. They thrust heads
through the wiring of their fence to nibble lawn
that stretched out ahead like understanding
while cryptic stands of fodder rustled behind.

After three weeks of grazing, the meadow showed signs
of altering into pasture. The high grass dwindled.
Raspberries receded, poison ivy vanished.
Sheep trails stole a march across the ground.
We'd wondered whether a mere dozen animals
could clear out half an acre in a month,
and by the end of June it was nearly done.
On Sunday morning when I brought their grain
all but one sheep ran up at the clank
of the feeding pail. He, a five-month's ram,
stood oddly, head hanging, clearly sick.
An hour later he lay thrashing on his side
spasmodic by the galvanized water tub.
One ear had dropped askew beside one eye
that rolled askew. "It's got into his brain.

Don't treat him rough or he'll go into convulsions,"
the veterinarian said, jabbing him with a needle.

Riding home in the truck the lamb stood gamely
as though facing down a ring of predators,
but he fell when the truck jittered over a pothole
and could not rise. We laid him in a stall
on a mattress of hay, watching him sink and groan
in spite of all attention. We poured water
down his soft throat from a Barbaresco bottle,
stuffed him with purges to push through the poison
that he had gobbled somewhere in the field.
We listened like nurses to his gurgled breath,
laying hands on his hot shaggy flanks, wondering
whether we had left anything undone
we might have done, aghast at being "fastened to
a dying animal." We had no gift
to heal the staggered lamb who had used himself
to help us even out a straggling meadow.
He gave us back his breath in an exchange
for what the meadow gave him, sprigs of laurel
that had lurked deadly in the undergrowth
and plucked his tongue, his brain, among the roses.

BARN FEVER

Nobody knows how much to make of barns,
certainly not a barn as old as this,
set in a farm too swampy and too rocky
to make you rich by cutting hay or grazing.
Our barn was built two hundred years ago—
the lower half. The beams are as old as that.
It probably held harness, kept a horse,
provided cover for a wagon or a pung
and, with boards laid across its crooked roofbeams,
gave half its upper spaces up to hay.
That was before the old house tumbled down
late in the eighteen-fifties. Its next owner,
Malachi * Andrews, who was much involved
in swapping land, begetting farmer's children,
or buying boats for sons who'd rather fish,
rebuilt the barn and then the house and buildings.

That was the golden age of barns. Three farms
were merged by Malachi into a hundred acres
of upland, stoneland, woodland, all to pasture,
mostly for cows. The new half of the barn
stood high enough for storing up salt hay
and sheltering ten milk cows underneath
in wooden stalls so expertly designed,
fitted and whitewashed, that the cow's manure
could be scraped out, without shifting a hoof,
to flow into a cave in the foundations.
The new house, proportioned like the new barn,
rested on masonry as crisp and solid
as the barn's own blocks of fitted Cape Ann stone.
Next to the barn old Malachi then built,
on slender granite pillars that held it off
the ground, a corncrib with dovetailed corners,
and, near the house, a root cellar and milkshed
to keep the milk and fresh churned butter cool.

* The Gloucestermen pronounced it "Mellicky."

For fifty years the barn stood at the center
of the traffic of the farm, above the house
to screen it from the wind. Malachi Andrews,
his offspring scattering from Essex to Salem,
kept up his walls to keep his cows from scattering,
bought lots for firewood, orchard, maple sugar,
and drove to Gloucester every market day.
At night the cows swallowed their cud in the barn.
When Malachi died Elizabeth soon followed.
Their sons went off to sea or to New Jersey,
and two of his daughters, one of them once married,
kept up the barn for two cows and some hens
with only twelve acres left them of the hundred.
They hired a man to help them cut their hay
in the salt marsh and float it up by dory.
They let the sparse old pastureland revert
to meadow. Crab apple and swamp maple
began to creep into the fields which once
had been held open by the force of farming.
One day the two old women, clearing brush,
started a fire to burn the slash, and one,
Miss Mary Brown, was not quite quick enough
to keep her long skirt out of the teeth of the flames
which caught her, brought her down. Her sister
lived on in the house a while but sold the cows.

In the thirty years that passed before I came
trees nudged in and advanced upon the barn.
The corncrib rotted and fell, the milk shed collapsed.
The hayloft in the barn, no longer needed
to keep the cattle fed, was subdivided
by two flimsy floors and turned into
a battery for hens, and the cattle stanchions
were strung with chicken wire. No repairs.
Two years more, and the chicken farmer's busted.

The house passed to a Harvard anthropologist
who built himself bookcases in a parlor
that up to then had been reserved for funerals.
He fitted out the kitchen with an electric stove,

dug in new plants around the house, and set
his mind to keeping up a large green lawn—
sure sign that the barn had now become
poor second to a house that was no more a farmhouse.
The anthropologist who tamed the grass
decided the country had become too tame
and sold the farmland to a State Street lawyer
who feared the devastation that would come
if some bad bolshevik laid nuclear waste to Boston.
His wife wallpapered in anticipation.

My first view of the farm: a day in March,
walking with friends down the field between dry stalks.
The barn's soaked black with last night's rain. Its south
wall gapes black with apertures, its eaves are piebald
with doors of nests for squirrels. The high roof,
shingled with asphalt by the chicken farmer,
has lost a number of its links, as though
the wind had tried to scale it like a fish.
Inside, someone's Mercedes. On a beam
two cooing pigeons have scuffled together
a shaggy nest in case of warmer times
for breeding, hatching. All around the barn
sumac and other thicketry are shoving
against the base of the walls, as though to nudge
the ancient building off its pins. The barn
has no friends left, it seems. Some boys have smashed
the floorboards upstairs where the chickens roosted.
If I'm to own it, how to heal the barn?

The house had been infected by the suburbs.
I heard the barn beside it heave a sigh
anticipating usufruct; or else decline,
decay, a sagging and senility;
or, worse, more merciless, a careless match
to send it up in flames like Mary Brown.
Nobody knows how much to make of barns
that do not shelter anything we value.
The crops are spent that went to Haskell's Mill.
This land has turned too sour even for hay

and lies now unprotected by the walls
that run and stumble, madmen, through the woods
which no one cuts or culls. Why are our barns,
that do not shelter anything we value,
left standing as an emblem of a past
when we owned things we thought more worth the keeping?
Sometimes in summertime our younger children
may hide and seek here to remember games
their great-grandparents used to play in barns—
but Malachi and Mary Brown did more than play.
They metamorphosed grass into milk and butter,
kernels and clamshells into hens and eggs,
dead seeds into the brightness of beans and corn.
Somehow the barn is all that they have left us.
What else is lingering on the land to press
its bristling, fading harvests in our arms?
The smells of milk, manure, and straw, a life
beyond the games suburban children play?
Time and some care have spared this barn, a sign
of the work a farm does to keep itself a farm.
Without the barn there would be little cause
to call this piece of land more than a piece
of land, one corner of it fastened down
by a yellow house where people sit and write
about the days when the farm had farmers on it
as well as the busiest barn for miles around.

SATAN IN GOATSKIN

Disarmed on the unhandy
side of the wall, I note
the stern end of the goat
whose forward mouth rips off
my unpicked brussels sprouts.
Lobbed rocks, berserker shouts
shock a stark staring goat into
thick-bodied parody of deer
with grace abounding,
vaulting and clearing
the fence. After which Nanny,
mistress of double-agentry,
bowing, browsing,
shifts shape from pestered
fugitive to pastured
livestock, safely sealed in by wire
with sheep unsafely grazing.
O goat, teetering
on manly hindquarters!
Mount up upon that rock!
O nibble, happy and murderous,
sweet sprigs of apple.
O girdle the boughs.
O kill the tree forever.
O ass-end to our house,
flip up your tail
like the flap of a pocket
and salute the master
who fenced you in his pasture.

FAWN

(for Sam and Jessica Warren)

Late summer dusk. Headlights along the road.
A sudden apparition by the hedge.
My car swerved aside of its own wish,
an instep arch crushed on the brake pedal,
and stopped in an instant. Jumped out
to learn whether we had killed anything
without a sound or click of contact.
Lying on asphalt, dazed but conscious,
half-lay a spotted fawn, so scrawny that
I could not tell whether it had been struck
by hunger, illness, or accident. Over one eye
a slight cut, slightly bleeding. The fawn
blinked, lay still. Now other cars were halting.
Occupants were out, shouting advice.
The fawn reclined, dreamy and indifferent.
After a quarter hour of altercation
we heaved the passive, lally-legged baby
into a van, one of us holding a head
that did not need the holding, wary of
the hooves that did not move or strike,
and settled it inside a neighbor's barn
with a sheep-nipple, evaporated milk,
chlorate of lime, a bottle, barley-sugar.
Out of all these warm deer-milk was concocted
and fed into the fawn with deep resistance
from one so weak, so wild, so uncomplaining.
Blowing into the corner of her mouth
triggered a reflex that would make her suckle
and take enough to help her stay alive:
most of the milk ran down along her neck
but some was kept. She lay with folded legs
unmoving, making no attempt to rise
when her feeders approached, not attempting
to give more than a sniff of cooperation.
The second day we took her from the barn
and fed her on the lawn. Her keeper let her go,
and suddenly she found her feet, making for open

country, so weak she could not navigate,
staggering sideways, legs scissoring.
Now, when we tried to put her in the barn,
she flailed out at us with those edged hooves
and struggled till we feared not for ourselves
but her, that she might shatter against the wall.
The third and fourth days she was so much stronger
that her tail flicked up and down when she was fed,
and she clattered back and forth in the dark stall.
We took her carefully into the sun,
fed her one last bottle, stood up and back,
and let her go. She walked, mincing forward,
then broke into a trot, and as we watched
she cantered down the lawn and onto the marsh,
tail held high, then out of view into the alders
that border on the marsh. There is no knowing
if she survived the winter, but it was a mild one.

JULY MEETING

Crow hollered, barking darkness like a trumpet.
Mockingbird followed, dragging behind
a ragbag of moonlit virtuosity.
Robin, at the shank end of mating season,
purled and knit the customary declarations.
Other "feathered songsters" waited,
treading air to hold position
till the loudest at length stood aside.
The cardinal's whistle faded.
Dawn song broke down
into twitter of sparrow and wren,
dove's coo, the receding
ball-peen strokes of oven-bird,
catbird's stuttering clauses.
Finally, after each
had said his grey say,
sun sprang from the edge of sky
into a vacuum of sound,
rewarding every ruddy tree,
calling the world to order.

THATCH

(Spartina alterniflora)

Thatch uncrouches
from the thick brown mat
of marsh like stubble
from the planet's beard,
edges to the seaward side
of its self-humbling cousin
spartina patens,
flourishes seeds overhead
at blade's length, and
flicks them free
into a tide as salt as tears.

PARADISE AS A GARDEN

(For Elizabeth B. Moynihan)

One of the great tautologies: self-regarding:
in which the seeds of growth
are the kernels of contemplation,
in which the contemplation of desire
ekes out desire's last sigh,
in which what enlarges the space
is its surrounding hedges:
husk and flower are one.

These were no northern sprawls, however,
no meadows of bluets and flax.
In Persia water collected itself, at whatever
cost, within walls: model of a house or city:
no water, no life. Yet sometimes paradise
persisted as boundaries only, and in the end
the garden stood, bracelets of stone and water,
without leaf, flower, or fruit to carry temptation.

And so it follows, through ages, crosses and tongues,
that when we speak of our eternal delight,
whether a garden we were once expelled from
or one that has been lost and overgrown,
it is the edges we cannot forget.
Whatever persists within, forever fresh,
is the indelible border of imagination.

ATMOSPHERES

(For Reg Saner)

1. *Boulder 1935*

Where the mountains lift from the plain
one of my boyhoods was toughened
in a stucco house, protected
by a palisade of lilacs,
purple one day in April,
the next bowed down in snow
that, melting, would uncover
red slate sidewalks
scribbled over with demotic
marks from children's rollerskates.

The snowflake came and went
in sparse Colorado air
that cracked the boards of pianos,
cooked eggs in cool water,
lifted cakes crankily,
stole away breath at hilltops,
and blotted stray moisture.

Oases? In one direction
the damp innards of Hanselman's
Greenhouse flaunted rainfall
orchids dangling from their roots.
In the other, the English throwback
of Mabel Reynolds' garden.
She ruled it, ramrod straight,
enunciating consonants like musketry
to repel the elisions of the West,
while her husband, Shakespearian George,
smiled on the world as though it were a theatre.

The surfaced streets held hard.
Air sizzled in the lungs.
Rocks and gravel abraded
a boy's bare knees despite

the vapors of campus life,
the cries of football crowds
that cheered for Whizzer White,
the oohs and aahs of tourists
at how the falling light
carved shadows in the cliffs
that westward and high upward
clamped down an early sunset
on days that seldom darkened
except with stormclouds or dust
that blew west from the poisoned plains.

2.   *Cheyenne Mountain 1944*

Ten boys of sixteen roped up
on a red crumbling cliff,
guided by a trigonometry teacher.
Climbing boots scuffed the rock,
catching enough edge to heave
bodies over the lip
of a squat ledge, each of us
breathing deep catches of air.
There! Stopped. There, there!
Above, just above. Clear eyes,
moonlit glass, nostrilly head
carrying a sweeping spiral
of horn—stock still, steady
as the rock whose arm he stood on,
a wild ram, bighorn!
Motion and sound both ceased.
When breathing again began
and with a sudden snort,
one of the boys snatched up
his geologist's pick. On wire thighs
he charged the ram. Who blinked,
breathed himself across the outcrops,
seesawed silently upward
and was inhaled by the landscape.
Our pursuer had to halt,
blinking through fogged glasses.

Now decades later, Gifford is dead,
and only a cramped gathering of bighorns
clusters above timberline.

3. *National Center for Atmospheric Research 1967*

The fortieth parallel flies around the world
as though launched from the ramparts
of I.M. Pei's mind-fortress. My first guide
to the site, an ancient mathematician,
limped through portals whose lintels
of ground-up mountain stone
glittered slightly with mica.
Below the mesa where the Center stands,
down there in the little city of the plain
where my flesh had flowered for women,
the air drooped thick with pollutants.
The old mathematician croaked out the terrible force
of the geometric progression. "There is no escape.
Population expands, stark as compound interest.
A penny invested by Caesar at simple interest
would be worth a few thousand today; but a penny
at compound interest earns gold
as massive as the planet."
Ieoh Ming's palatial Chinese puzzle
sprouts from the flank of the foothill
like a dusty mushroom. Doorways shackle
vistas of the plains, unimpeded sights
of the sky, green-robed, pink-tinted mountains.
Glass in the windows is tinted
just enough to admit
all elements of the light except glare,
brilliance without dazzle.
Under the molded cover of the walls
unearthly silicon chips,
linked into computer circuits,
monitor the winds of the world
while at their side sit men and women
lightly breathing. Their house

of inquiry shelters without surprise
the earth's commotion, while
the chinook breathes warmly
on dissolving snow.

4.   *Boulder 1979*

Where the mountains lift from the plain
I work beside a woman
in kerchief and rounded apron.
We extricate earthenware
from the racks of her kiln.
Her dishes, once moist clay,
now cool and hard as agate,
open their rough-scalloped
rims skyward to swallow
whatever happens to be served
on their surfaces. Flakes of snow
hiss lightly on the glazes
and gather into drops
that the empty air will inhale.

We carry our unfired flesh
through atmospheres and climates
that wait for our decay,
expecting things alive
to take on the life of things.
Change drifts down on our heads
from a past mediated
by mason, shaman, priest—
all those who learned the secret
that the seed must be buried to live,
caught up in atmospheres,
loosening into vapor,
tightening into snowflake.

IL SE SAUVE

"He saw that he had lost his fear of falling
and all other fears of that nature." JOHN CHEEVER

More like a well than a dungeon,
more like a cave than a jail,
the cell shows shadow figures on its wall.
Can such semblances of truth keep
men captive closer
than whip-wielding mistresses
and swag-belted sheriffs? The convicted
tumble into their own preparations—
punjjis, nooses, petards.
Every teaspoon of punishment has been anticipated.

Saints and prisoners embrace such exercises as
pushups, double-entry computations,
mnemonics, and other apportionments.
They write about pilgrims, knights-errant,
victims of illusion. All they need
to expose the vast illusion of prisons
is the wings of an angel.

Even a peregrine's flight may be bribed.
A falconer deceives his hawk with a hood
to which she surrenders in an orderly sequence
of decisions, becoming accustomed
to jesses, gantlets, darkness,
gobbets of dead meat,
rations of light and flight.
The falcon, no angel,
chooses to submit.

The cell itself becomes the enemy.
To accept the minimum security of life,
wings must fall from the shoulders.
Among shadows and sentences you remember
when you could have made a break for it,
when, if you had had the wings of an angel,
you could have got out of here,
uplifted, saved yourself.

TWO MIDRASHIM

1. *Untuned String* (PSALM 90)

> *"Yea, the work of our hands, establish thou it."*

My childhood Steinway spoke in tongues
(*Liebesleid, lacrimae rerum, ostinato*)
when other people played it.
Sometimes a visitor—Lhevinne, Sykes, Raieff—
could make the family instrument talk turkey,
but when I perched up tight between its legs
my stubby fingers whacked out sounds
that broke the bright charge of music.

O god in the machine! You have cast
a penumbra of sound across all memory,
the purple garment of Europe I wear,
my American secret. And you strike
an even darker note: something's amiss with my hands.
I can carry a tune only with voices.
Never fit to manage
the nineteenth century's noblest invention,
(the one that enabled mere men
to establish the work of their hands)
I am shut out from taking a hand in sonatas,
dismissed from polonaise, mazurka, prelude, fugue,
mordant, glissando, thoroughbass.
I may not harrow music with my hands.
I'm struck dumb by a pentecost of piano.

2. *Darkheart* (JOB 19:26)

The scientist of the night
and the walker in the city
convey me, one at each elbow,
over the shadows of anger
toward my unwillingness.
Wakeful and stiff,
I glower in the darkness
with eyes that will not aid
my body to seek the light.

How graceless to deny
that grunt of understanding:
that only *in my flesh*
shall I see God!

THE LAUGHTER OF WOMEN

When men go out for laughs, they give their all,
baring their teeth, betraying no memory
of the slave quarters, master's rumpled bed,
heaps of hacked corpses at the river crossing,
bodies bent back in alleyways or gardens.
Men's voices rise and sharpen nasally
to slice even their brothers off at the knees,
ho-hoing at the gallons of booze, the babes
the other put away the night before.
"Hey Roy, better shut your eyes
before you bleed to death."

The laughter of women holds a world at bay,
whether through giggles of girls leering askance
at the hulking narcissistic strut of an athlete,
or with the hushed laughter of a fiancée
feeling a stranger's eyes stroking her breasts,
or in the stylized *ha-ha* of zarzuela dancers
(hand on one hip, flower in the teeth,
wrist flung overhead like a whiplash).
Laughter gives women strength, protection, help,
making men wonder what their secret is.

"We know your ways," men hear that laughter say.
"As girls we bathed and dressed boy babies
and cannot disremember what you are.
Though swaying to your sex, should we not fear
that love will promptly turn away its face
the day we trust you to implant a life?
To make light of man's yoke, that costly burden,
we laugh at the dark, the dark that pulls us down."
The laughter of a woman is her pride.
Men smile and shake their heads to think of it,
how gladly women wear their rings, their houses.
The heads of women lean together, laughing.

FROM

A VOICE IN THE MOUNTAIN

(*1977*)

*And he said, Go forth, and stand upon the mount
before the Lord. And, behold, the Lord passed by,
and a great and strong wind rent the mountains, and
brake in pieces the rocks before the Lord; but the
Lord was not in the wind: and after the wind an
earthquake; but the Lord was not in the earthquake:*

*And after the earthquake a fire; but the Lord was
not in the fire: and after the fire a still small voice.*

*And it was so, when Elijah heard it, that he wrapped
his face in his mantle, and went out, and stood in the
entering in of the cave. And, behold, there came a
voice unto him, and said, What doest thou here, Elijah?*

I KINGS: 19:11–13

THE POEM IN THE PARK

She waited eagerly on a park bench,
holding in her arms the humming of the day,
her eyes welling with *lacrimae rerum*.
I walked toward her through the bricky streets,
tasting as I came the sky of the public park,
its gates ajar, its paths cast wide in welcome,
the bench warm beside her
with the words the poem and I would engage together.
But as I walked in under the sighing trees,
a gust of wind scattered from the dark pond
a flock of mallards, wings whistling,
crying out and fanning toward the harbor
over the buildings between the park and the sea.

Not till hours later, hemmed in between
office telephone and office typewriter,
did it come back to me. I'd left the poem
seated motionless upon a wooden bench
with tears in its eyes.

LA BOCCA DELLA VERITÀ

The little piazza called the Mouth of Truth after the
big marble face of the sun in the church portico, whose
mouth was supposed to snap shut if you put your hand
in it and told a lie, but which was perhaps an ancient
sewer lid . . . ELEANOR CLARK, *Rome and a Villa*

I thrust my fingers, crossed in an artful lie,
into the mouth of truth, the fluid of sex,
the darkness of death, murmuring tuneful noises.
The porch of a church ought to be good for a gamble.
In front, the face of the sun. Behind, the temples,
one round, Tempio di Vesta, home and hearth,
one square, Tempio della Fortuna Virile.
Both sexes call on us to tell the truth.

If I speak out, will doves and bluebirds descend
and the butterflies of the world slip their leashes?
If I tell, will tigers carry me to Tibet
or elect me poet-priest of a sunlit island?
I have turned away from the pleaders
and pretended to be asleep.
Only a stone's throw from Cloaca Maxima
I cringe in the lap of the great goddess,
shrinking from these monumental Roman exertions.
Who asked my soul to magnify the Lord?

Take the right hand. Place it in the sun's mouth.
If art is not "a lie that tells the truth,"
why else, except in aid of some good God,
should I hope to tell the world my kind of lie
and not be swallowed by a river of darkness?

I dare to pledge my powers to the sun.
How coldly will the marble give its answer?
If I have truly lied in the mouth of truth
let my right hand forget her cunning.

ZENITH: WALKER CREEK

1. *Head Stone*

The great rock blazes high above the marsh.
From its highest foothold my father's ashes were scattered.
Much lordlier than any human chieftain,
the cliff allows high tides to lick its foot
and gathers pines around it like a blanket.
When I'm asleep, as well be dead as absent
from weather and the rock. The trees, unpruned,
squeeze out new shoots despite all seasons' endings.
The compost seethes beneath its quilt of straw.
In the autumn, sun springs up in the grass but freezes,
halted by dark winds jostling from the mountains
to kindle maple, sumac, beech and oak
into cold standards gorged erect with flame.
The land is all I'm given to imagine.
In absences I might as well be dead,
a vole's trig corpse beneath the currant bushes.
What goes on, gone? Friends die. Some few of them
dispatch themselves. It happens in their rooms
and books, in blankets, in their buried beds,
the bedrock of their basements, in their graves.
The rock, in presence or in absence, glows
like old love letters. It endures, no matter,
when no more dreams are stirring on the farm
and no true feeling leaves no memory.

2. *Bicentennial*

The cinquefoil in the field
stands up to yellow clover,
strawberries, hawkweed,
daisies almost over.

Swallows dive and swoop;
they tremble, glide and roll.
Necklaces of wren-song
chatter down the stone wall.

Roses stud the edge of the woods
where goldenrod is growing.
Ovenbirds are teaching.
Cattle might be lowing

were trees not making motions
to wipe our fields away.
Two hundred years of farming?
A single stand of hay.

3.   *Making Much of Orioles*

Teetering high in the feathers of an elm,
two orioles chortled halfway into spring
while their green cover faded into dun,
breasting the normal current of the season.
The tree trunk bled wet life into the ground.
Dutch elm disease. The tree had been no beauty,
strangled in its early days by grapevine,
embraced by poison ivy, tickled by thistles;
yet when it was felled an unfamiliar light
erased familiar shadows from the garden.

I walked around the tree to count the branches
that must be lopped before the trunk could be
bucked into cordwood. Here, suspended sideways,
a pouch of gray silk dangled, gave out peeping.
Three chicks inside, as featherless and bright
as oranges, crouched back and yawned in my face.
Parental discord rang from nearby willows.

Maybe the nest could be removed, like houses
that block the highway, crawling on a trailer,

or bob behind a tugboat, buoyed and hawsered
betwixt the fishing villages of Newfoundland.
I pruned the dangling branch that held the nest
at its tip, like moss wrapped round a finger,
and cradled it along a ladder, stretched
as high up a chokecherry tree as I could reach,
fifty feet short of normal oriole altitude.
The chicks kept cheeping, fearful for their balance
when borne by clumsy hands and not the wind.
With every knot I wound another tie
between the elm branch and the cherry tree,
hanging the nest too high for predators.

Now for the parents, fixated on elms.
They hovered frantically near the supine tree
in search of the family they'd left dangling,
three chicks too small to fly, a nest
redoubtable enough to brave the elements.
How to believe that house could simply vanish
to rebuild in an unfamiliar tree?
I waited, sometimes whistling their calls,
a mocking-man who sang in dialect.
It might—or not—have been an accident
that before sundown the elders took their nest
at cherry value, unfamiliar height,
with chicks inside that must have been their own.
For several weeks I watched them come and go,
mother or father fetching food, while one
sang unto heaven in a higher tree.
The elm-leaves grew brown and dry and dead,
but twine still bound elm to the darker cherry
while, in the nest, the chicks gained flying weight.

One morning in July the nest was empty.
The younger and the older birds had gone:
parents and children roamed the world together.
The withered nest hung on, now limp, a trophy
of something like a victory of will.
I climbed the ladder to untie my knots

and hung the dried branch with its tattered flag
on the wall of my room, perhaps to hatch its meaning.

But a nest is no place to arrest a song
that in its very nature has no end.
The second year the orioles found an elm
to build in somewhere in the neighborhood.
They might have been my nestlings. I don't know.
I've tossed the branch behind a lilac bush.

4.   *Zenith: Walker Creek*

The woodcock now spends his evenings more quietly.
The robin sings less urgently, more chirpy.
Grass which sprang up for a while as though
it meant to reach the stars each afternoon
has moderated its ambitions a little.
The fields have settled down to heavy feeding and breeding.
Marsh, its winter khaki conquered,
has greened itself into equator color,
swaying taller and taller with the tides' tickling.
"Nature's first green is gold." Her second
is opaque as billiard tables. Now she plays her game,
less urgency in the dawns, less melodrama.
The pheasant's declaration rings out half as often;
the minnows flutter calmly in their pools,
having learned their prey cannot escape.
The shade is deeper, more desirable.
Dogs trot in preference to running,
spend more of daylight sprawling and panting.
The pedalling bicyclists shift to lower gears,
the bay blooms with looser and larger sails.
Our sun has given of its best in waxing:
It teeters above our heads as nearly
as the earth's escapism will permit,
toppling with some reluctance after noon
toward the West to keep us on the boil
till the anger of flies and the hunger of mosquitoes
drive us from sun to shade, from shade to the shelter

of screens, where, after fall of darkness, we drown
our senses in sunburn, poison ivy, gin.
Drinking deep, hot-headed, we sleep dark.
Those long days were the promises we broke.

5. *Day Of Wrath*

September silence sags over the field.
Faded summer denims flap with fatigue
on a neighbor's clothesline.
No birds sing, only crickets and katydids.
Yesterday the heaven twittered with swallows;
today at noon the wires are swept empty
of occupants. From an enormous distance
the crow cries out his carrion comfort.
The pasture, lately mowed, noses aside yellow bristles
with a new cropspill of bluegreen autumn blades.
The sun sizzles on rocks, striking raisinly wrinkles
into the unpicked grapes, which white-tailed hornets
ignore, to feast on the drowsy flies
who do not hear them coming.
The marsh tides move like syrup.
Their dark water stirs the seed-heavy grasses
like masts of sloops at anchor.
Beechnut hulls bristle under the
toughening hats of their leafage.
Gardens have been harvested of beans and corn.
The dry soil flourishes mostly with immigrants:
brussels sprouts, broccoli, *aubergines, poireaux*.
Shortening days turn crisp after nightfall.
By day the air still hums with the sound of sleep.
This afternoon is tangled in its silence
until a yellow dog, posted to guard an empty house,
lets out a howl. His desertedness will never end.
No man will cross the road for his relief.
His work of watching will go on forever.

6. *Cross Cut*

Slumped on a pallet of winter-withered grass
you lie dead at my feet, in age not quite
a century, perhaps, but twice as old as I am,
in a pose your twisted trunk and dwindling leaves
had never hinted, even at your sickest.
How many stubs your gangrened upper branches
had turned into sockets and armpits
for squirrel, coon and starling
to burrow in! You thrust erect as stiff
as the memory of my oldest neighbor who watches
each new spring for your fluttering bloom
and every August for a pride of pears—
green to the eye, woody to the tooth,
taut and cidery to the fumbling tongue.
For years we've watched you dying from the top,
a peril to climbing children and seekers of shade,
but knew that, pear-like, you could stand for years,
heart eaten out, just fingering your life.
Perhaps I could have helped you out of the air
with some shreds of your stature left intact,
but now I've failed you. You lie invisible
behind the wall, your most disgraceful branches
lopped and hauled for firewood, resting scarred,
beyond your element, crushed by your own weight,
shapeless and pitiful as a beachbound whale.
Only inches above the nourishing ground
a cross-cut stump, stark white, reveals at bottom
you're still as lively as the day you bloomed.
The hearts of your leaves shone out in valentines
and your windborne, lilting, sinewy boughs
heaped proudly up toward the waning sun
those glowing, softly tinted, bumper bushels.

7. *Thanksgiving*

(For Gunilla Jainchill)

By the authority vested in me, a gift,
(in German, *poison*; in Swedish, *a marriage*)
I write of journeys, placenames, interventions,
inheritances visible, alive, dead.
A milkweed pod atop its autumn stalk
bulges from cold and flips itself wide open.
It sprinkles flurries of snow between the grassblades
to bloom, mulberry-like, for next midsummer,
nourished by milk no bitterer, no whiter
than any I have tasted as a gift.

8. *Skiing By Moonlight*

Orion reclines on his hip.
Polaris glares high at my left.
I glide my way homeward,
a quarter-moon chasing me.

We follow the lurching shadow
of my sweaty body back
along the newly-crumbled tracks
I slogged only an hour ago

through the mirror-image pasture.
(Polaris twinkled at my right,
Orion teetered at my left;
the moon, narrow as a candle,

sparkled on smooth, blameless snow,
a beach of diamonds.
Cedars were heaped with treasure
among frozen cherry trees.)

Our sheep have all taken shelter
within the black barn.
In the windless moonlight
only an owl hoots against the cold

while deer, silent among pines,
wait to hear my skis stop hissing
and the back door click shut

before they wade toward the rick
to steal some hay.

HASKELL'S MILL

Legend foams up around this farmlike place
that looks both landward and toward the tides
whose surf is hammering behind the hill.
Tales are written of an abandoned gristmill,
"one of the first tidal mills in the New World,"
that cooled the heels of a hundred Union soldiers
parching in bivouac one summer day:
"Their captain marched them down to the creek
at high tide and off the mill dam, in columns."
It stood within eyeshot of this very house.
Almost a hundred years ago the mill
produced its final particle of flour.
With no compacted power in the waters
a mill's no better than a ruined city,
a pencil mark beside the illiterate tides.
Still, we remember. There's a little left
of Haskell's Mill, "the remains of the dam, some rocks
and waterlogged timbers." The Haskells had been given
"the license of the town in 1690
to build this tide mill for grinding corn.
The tide was high enough there, certainly,
to make a pool of every incoming tide.
The controlled outflow turned the water wheel.
Vessels are claimed to have docked here
to take on meal for the West Indies trade." *

Do we remember? The books remind us, and
beside the creek where boys still dig for worms
they all recall the spot as "Haskell's Mill."
A ruined skiff rots by the waterside.
The yellowlegs and plover scream in voices
anxious with autumn, with migration coming.
High tide pours in, kingfishers skim the pool,
crabs nibble at the rising of the tide,
and gulls search hopefully along the brink
only to flap away where fancy calls.
At the far end of a sloping stony track

* Joseph E. Garland, *The Gloucester Guide*, 1973

the shingled house of food stood by the water.
The center post, the thickness of a tree,
bore up the millstones, grooved and geared to grind
opposed, in and out of disengagement,
governed by pulleys and levers with hickory handles
to make the slab stones kiss and scour each other.
At every touch white flour puffed and drizzled
down through a funnel in the nether stone
to rise, like bleached sand in an hourglass,
until the hopper filled, and then the mealsacks,
and then the lighters shuttling to the ship
to weigh anchor, to set sail for the islands.

The millstones now lie buried in the ground,
doorsteps for the houses of two neighbors,
Parsons and Roberts, who had not been born
the day the stones cracked the last grain of wheat
and lapsed into disuse and passive silence.
The tide seizes and rattles fists of stone
at random. We've withdrawn allegiance
from land and sea. We take our pay from strangers,
unthinkable during the two hundred years
when Haskell's Mill encouraged every farmer
to drag his wagonload to the waterside.
The Mill served children as a diving platform
for the mill-pool's swimming hole, and then it was gone.
All the wheatfields that catered to its stones
are built up or grown over. The farms are woodland,
sprinkled with cars that have been left for dead
after carting city people to a country
where nothing is produced and little earned.
The neighbors marry, hold a job, and keep
their land in hopes developers will buy
to spare them the indignity of ruins.

Not even rumor can recall the miller,
the ruler of the cropland and the marsh,
a figure standing in a primal world
that planted crops and turned them into meal

without the use of any other force
than the human mind and nature in her seasons.
He served in an apron crusted stiff with flour
while water howled and millwheels groaned and trembled.
He held the balance between sea and land,
the sun and moon, the water and the stone.

THE FALL OF THE DOLLS' HOUSE

The family figurines sat round a fire
at the hearth of a dolls' house, porcelain-faced,
dove-breasted, leaning against each other,
smiling as though their rage were ruled by music,
the transcendental chords of Plato's dream.
Father, a kindly provider, judge, and priest,
Mother, a milkmaid, mending things, healing,
Children at play, at rest, reading their lessons—
such are the lessons that our lessons taught.
A window-frame hemmed in this perfect scene
for all to worship, as we worship icons.

Beside the dolls' house that the family built
the father's drunk. His wife weeps for her sex.
Young Tim is crippled and will surely die.
The older children dream of rape and murder,
for which of them has strength enough to act
as ancestor? The dolls' house shows them how
all parents fail, the Virgin fails the Child.
Their icon topples before war, change, chaos;
embraces yield to riots in the streets.
The pulse beats hard when Manson or Attila
kicks in the fire door, wrestles down Papá,
mugs mother, rapes the girl, snaps like twigs
the GI crutches of poor Tiny Tim.

Look at the dolls' house my grandparents owned
(its furniture imported from Saxe-Coburg)
in this contented photo. In another
the harmony of Diderot and Newton
takes on the dissonance of Marx and Freud.
My parents' glamor hints a naughty streak:
their dolls wear knickers, camisoles, bandeaux.
In a more recent snap, my wife and I,
nurtured on Tillich, Kierkegaard, Jung,
wear casual clothes but strike a mannered pose.
I slouch eccentric, while she smiles, protecting

the children underneath a cherry tree.
We'll leave the house, I think. The leaves are falling.

My children see themselves as in a poster:
unisex, well-provided, amplified.
Shatter the house, my darlings, helter-skelter!
The harmonies of our philosophy
have let us sleep through years of cuckoo-clocks
in drawing-rooms of matchsticks, cards, and lace.
If you are granted wishes for the world,
enlarge its scope: make work as one with play
in houses built for everlasting fire
where man and woman burn like seraphim.

OFFISSA POPP

A Maneuver in Class Warfare

My father suited up
for two world wars
but was never recruited
to clean a weapon:
officer material.
Between wars he fancied
firing a borrowed shotgun
at (or near) birds.
But once a pheasant
whom he had stunned
and left me to carry
came undone.
Father strode on
gunning and missing.
His bird woke up
and stared me down.
The two of us sat
in the stubbled cornfield.
That was that.

One war later
he took up skeet.
His pals at the range
kept his twelve-gauge shiny;
but when he made
his big move to town
the gun was cleaned,
packed up, broke down.

A third war came
along, and I
went off to do
my hitch—G.I.
On my discharge
my father pleaded
he badly needed
his shotgun cleaned.

He needed it now
but he didn't know how.
As a boy whose mother
had never let him bother
with guns or other
store-bought mayhem,
I wondered why
a former G.I.
should serve this two-time fat man
as a batman?

Duty scoured the Winchester
with patches and rods.
Apologizing to the gods
of war, I poured,
and smeared the pad
with olive oil
(nothing else on hand)
and scrubbed out the gun
in pride and pity,
preserving the citi-
zens' right to bear
arms, by hiding a piece
like an adulterer's underwear
behind the galoshes
in a sixteenth-floor closet
on Fifty-seventh Street
in New York City.

Oh I polished the gun
he thought he might flourish
but he never assembled it
before he passed on.
When his executor
sold it for a pittance,
it was lubricated all right.
The bore shone bright.
An enlisted man's fate
is to clean his gun

before he may eat.
I should have beat-
en the thing into
a goddam plowshare.

THE COMPOUND EYE

(For L. E. Sissman, 1928–1976)

What an intolerable deal of history!
You were the fly upon a thousand walls,
the poet's eye with many hundred lenses,
master of every curiosity.
Marked down for death, nipped early at the heels,
you walked with shambling evasion, not in a hurry,
too proud to betray the merest smudge of panic.
Yet in your poems death lies never far
from the surface, knife beneath the water,
dark age pending. To stay alive for it
tubers and relics of each season's growth
must be tucked into order, time, and place.
Familiar phrases bowed beneath strange burdens
("a pleasure dome of Klees and Watteaus made"),
pleasures of a couplet coupled with
the nausea of chemotherapy.
Amid the disorder of illness, dying, death,
you put in order your arrested life.

Go, prince: peer owlish through the windowpane
betwixt the daintiness of your imagination
and all the tawdriness and disarray
our life is dressed in. From the postwar city
look out at the city of God, and then confess
how sweet was the disorder in the dress.

LA CATHÉDRALE ENGLOUTIE

An ancient place. The roofs are high and grey.
A friend and I walk down a cobbled street.
I've never seen an alleyway so neat:
brisk brooms have swept each speck of dust away.

No motor, tire or wheel makes hiss or clatter
across the squares or past the whitewashed angles.
My friend says, "poor and rich agree: no wrangles!
Here nothing has ever seemed to be the matter."

In the cathedral square the Church stands fast:
its leaded panes of red and blue depict
a squad of sturdy saints, with spires erect
unsmirched by soot or by iconoclast.

Within, black hats and furled umbrellas press
past chapels of mahogany, toward cages
that stand behind the apse, to bank their wages
and scribble checks where sinners once confessed.

Observe the great south aisle, the Bishop's Tomb:
walk out into the nave. No monk or priest
makes antiphon, and no one kneels. From east
to west a flock of tables fills the room,

and banqueters participate in revel.
They dance and drink from foamy steins of beer
between the speeches. How they love to hear
that cash has saved the country from the devil!

"Listen, my friend, what made your family chafe
to live in any other town? Why here?"
We walk in silence through another square.
"The schools are good," he sighs. "The streets are safe."

TOWARD AN UNDERSTANDING OF
THE PUBLIC LIFE

The President, my father, and myself
drove out along Route 6. Dog came for the ride.
The President had just resigned. Father was some years dead.
The President was clearly loth
to attract public notice. No one in the car
except for Dog had much to say to Nixon,
but otherwise we travelled pretty easy.
In mid-Cape Cod a tire blew out. The Pres-
ident was amazed, for in High Office such
things hardly ever happen. He refused to dismount.
Nothing for me but to hoof it, lugging a three-gallon can.
I found no filling-stations open (the roads
were crowded with traffic attending Gaudí cathedrals)
but I did locate a garage, sited where two one-way
streets began: where cars might leave but not enter.
Our options exhausted, we abandoned the car
and checked ourselves into a small hotel
where tongue-and-groove planks line the corridor,
floors dark with rust-and-green linoleum.
Here we lodge to this day: my father dead and silent,
Dog an unregistered guest. I observe
and record the President's words. He paces his room
insisting on his innocence and our guilt.

THE DIAMOND PIPE

(For Dan Jacobson)

Fumbled out of the earth
by what sluices and clay-clotted fingers,
plucked under the stern-eyed faces
of inspectors and watchmen,
breathlessly guarded, sorted, parcelled out
in walled and fanged secrecy
among cramped artisans for cutting and polishing,
this heap, this sandpile, this burnished pipe
of jewels lie, scatterlights,
facet and mirrored subfacet, lurking inside the dark hall
while alarms and chains hold back the surge of the crowd.

Opening time. The greatest show on earth,
the most sublime ingathering of light,
the most singular collection of the most
precious stones from the largest
diamond pipe ever tapped,
draws queues and columns of gawkers
to line the block in ranks while the cars
of millionaires draw to the curb
for the opening. The lights are about to go on.
Resting upon their cushions of black and scarlet velvet,
the gems have done their work, completed their
struggle for survival, finished their vegetable thrust
toward the light. Water, food, fertilization were all
accomplished millions of years ago.
They of all living things are the survivors.
They lie in the dark in silence
awaiting adoration.

CREATURES OF THE GENITIVE

(For Frances Lindley)

Adjectives of desire, knowledge, memory, power,
fullness, sharing, and guilt take the genitive.
RULE OF LATIN GRAMMAR

Something lay hidden deep within the mountain.
I don't know what. Perhaps it could be love,
although I heard reports that thirsty tigers
had skulked around the heights in search of water
and startled tourists, full of food and wine,
exciting fear and other kinds of tension.

No wonder dreams like mine gave rise to tension
beyond whatever talk one heard of tigers.
What the high country left me with was love.
It followed me to settle near salt water,
but dreams went on for years beneath the mountain,
and memories as dizzying as wine.

The palate seldom has enough of wine,
but excess of indulgence heightens tension
so that your thirst transcends the power of love
to slake, a guilt as terrible as tigers.
A hundred strolls around our homely mountain
in quest, in endless quest, of crystal water

(O how dry country troubles you with water!)
brought me up short, or face to face with tigers
near brooks or lakes half up (or down) the mountain.
I tell you, I have had my share of tension.
Beneath the heights where all the world drinks wine,
two can afford the luxury of love.

One's second guess would have to be that love,
a thing as precious as untasted wine,
whether it wear the form of rocky mountains
or the transparent coverlet of tension,
is what the heart seeks when it desireth water.
But try to tell that to a thirsty tiger.

85

The hunger of the soul's a dream of tigers
mauling and snarling. Blunt their fangs with wine,
kiss knowledge in a whirlwind, crawl toward water,
trifle with fire and earthquake, piss on love,
lose nerve in each entanglement with tension—
and still a small voice murmurs in the mountain.

Though memory tenses with the guilt of tigers,
knowledge, desire, and love share sweetest water
when the strong mountain fills itself with wine.

FROM

WALKING THE BOUNDARIES

(*1974*)

ASKING NOTHING

The words carry themselves as carefully
as a muscular woman tricked out in sequins
walking a high wire.
I ask nothing of them, I only
set them in motion as gently as feathers.
Birds exert themselves more than the words do.
Hunger compels them, they cannot choose but fly.
Words, who seek no food for themselves,
follow a leader they have not chosen
in an order they have hit upon without deciding.
Only those words are admitted that speak of their speaker.
Whether they speak well or ill of me
is not their business nor even mine.
Their only need is, they should speak a language.
Having walked a way, they return to silence,
leaving only the memory of the drum-roll,
the sequins, the spotlight, the high wire.

DOORS

I know what lies behind them in the attic.
I have been filling its dusty corners for years.
Those pigskin suitcases, with ancient labels
from Karlsbad or København, no longer fit
even for storing woollens, have been covering
for the wrong man.
Toys with a leg broken,
cartons of dead letters, not one of these
means a thing now except as part of me.

I am bursting, dying.
My body is broken.
The rooms might be as empty without me
as they are already empty of the dead;
and I am even emptier than the rooms,
for I contain them.
I am not a plant, I am dying.
There is no bud-time for me, no seed-time.
I am a chieftain without a tribe,
a lover without a bed.
My arms fly at my side, my knuckles pop.

A woman is listening to me.
She leans forward, sets her hand on my knee.
Her eyes shine.
She listens, she understands.
I cannot do it without her.
Pascal said the greatest fear in life
is the fear of sitting quietly in a room alone.

I peer up the stairs. I strike a note.
There is no one there to see, to hear,
under the rafters. The loneliness
in this last room is infinite.
I have shut my past in here
behind the doors I have closed,
and all the rooms contain me.

THE HEROINE

She was one of the few I can speak of who believed
in personal destiny; the only one who swore
by holy writ that death was worth gambling on;
the meanest spirit to claim a martyrdom
since sainthood ended. What a cunning braggart
she was, a frailty who pictured herself
as a rider of skis, of waves, of men, of horses.
She lugged about a pessary in her purse
like a baloney sandwich in a lunchbox
and referred to Dylan Thomas and Dostoevski
in the tone of voice reserved for former lovers.
Breck hair, white scarves, clean flesh, hard muscles,
sun-worship, and a trough of molten and remorseless work.

I've seen her love-letters—those she wrote
to other men while she was using me—
and her hate-letters—those she wrote
to me while she was using them—but only once
or twice her tiny writing in a different hand,
tilted across the page, wounded, but credible
as the early morning trail of half an earthworm,
speaking of her selfhood in the tiny voice
that had been hers as a child, hers once as a girl, hers, hers.
In the usual rooms she spoke in a voice more humble
than the one she wrote in, cozening her larynx
to belie the costumes of ambition, clothes
Mother had dressed her in to go to school.
In saddle shoes and pageboy bob, disguised
as Betty Boop, inculcable, unresisting,
she set out bait for poets and professors.
She was as innocuous as Lenin in Switzerland.

The acrid sun tugs at her shrinking skin.
Out in the desert, blankeyed from deceptions,
she hugs herself to herself, learns how to ride,
to hate, to write, to broadcast, to give milk.
Her husband and her children, grating on her,
teach her a little more of how humans do it,

of how humanity must learn to sleep.
But then the tiny voice within her voice
struck up its canticle of loathing for
ambition's wigs and masks. Off with disguises!
Snarling and sobbing like an orchestra,
she levelled the forests of ego,
whirling around her bare blonde head
a sword as holy as a samurai's.

EMBRACES

1. *The First Stranger*

She wants his way! He's won! His will, set free,
canters inside his head, and fingers grip;
she nestles close, suggests with tooth and lip
the time is past for play;
her hands, the bolder pair, direct his way;
he is astonished at such avidness,
shrugs out onto the plain of nakedness
to find her there, an offering; he nears
what cannot be reversed; he summons in
his wits to guide his memory and smears
bookish caresses on her stranger skin
until her breath reminds him: it is She.

2. *Stranger Still*

Puffed like a silken sleeve, your body
dimples under my sausage fingers
as we give over to double dreaming,
slithering over each other in silence,
except for the sound of separate gasping,
to give it to each other here, this body
I call mine grappling with the one you call yours,
wrapped in summer sheets, wet
with sweat and (soon to be) with semen,
giving it, giving it, giving it
to the humped and whimpering stranger
who soon will lie beside me, knowing only
I too am wet, I too am awake.

3. *Family Reunion*

Dreaming of scattering mists, I awake
to the warmth of a breathing and browsing.
My hand is touched. A shoulder tingles.
A breast is tapestried over with hair.
No dream, no dream.
Our bed puts by the fragrance of sleep
to take on the liquor and odor of waking.
The hand rambles. I swim out of myself
into the welcoming lake of your flesh.
Fractiousness and the humdrum spatter
of chattels and children
of meals and mercy
go shying away.
Our bones go begging, breathing like bells.
We rise through the plaster ceiling,
majestic as two full moons,
till, far off, tenderly as a heron circling,
unaware that a footfall has been chosen,
we drift back through the bivouacs of darkness,
breathing easy.
We alight on the earth,
enter the house,
sigh deep down into the dens of our bodies.

BED TIME

Few beds are stonier than one shared by a sleeper
and a waker who stares into the dark
listening to the house breathe. Children
sigh, dogs snore, clocks tick, radiators mutter.
Love past, he lies vacant. Bed carries him
to countries that his body will never visit,
regions where his mind cannot drink the water.

Feet up. Blood trickles through his head
to pass between Horn Gate and Ivory Gate.
Sleep pilot, dreamer, flying Dutchman,
he steers his ticktock course between chills and fever,
bound out of Birthport for Lovepool and Death Haven.

Love past! Clandestine beds in borrowed apartments.
Fern beds, pine needles, beds for *porcheria,*
beds whose springs crumpled from exuberance
or rattled with anger, beds whose backs bent
from nightly throes of union and reunion.
"O bed, where first I loosed my virgin girdle . . ."
She fell upon her knees and kissed the bed.

As in a hospital where he awaits in bed
the next day's condescension of doctors,
he bleeds broken promises. Is it sailing time
for the ship of fools, the ship of the dead?
Pain lightning flickers and spatters
the four-cornered flatland of his life,
but what else is there to fall back on?
In bed we depend upon nothing but bed.

THE DANCE OF THE HOURS
or, *It's a Living*

Each hour of workaday fits just as well
as my old tweed jacket which has taken years
to learn to sag its shoulders. Sixty thousand
hours have rubbed up this telephone, tattooed
the roller of the typewriter. O shelves
and drawers, what purple uprisings you've stacked
into submission! For you I've herded papers
in and out to be disposed of elsewhere—
say in the crypt, say in the dead file.
I cling to my perch between the two baskets,
what a responsible spot. I'm here to keep
things that come *In* from getting *Out* too soon.
No one will liberate those memoranda
ranked up behind their fellows in the file
unless it be the moth that flickers, remembering
the odor of our bargain. We've forged a set
of deeds, wills, seasons, my hours and I.
We grow together in one tree, sparing and spending.
We never speak of what has passed between us.
We stare at one another through a window
and wonder which will be the first to sell.

IN THE SEVENTIES

1. Is Anything Wrong?

(For Margaret Atwood)

I do not know what I mean. Perhaps you know.
These lilypads, these ghostly gingkos and herons
stretch up their presences from the anti-world.
I live and move among visions; I hold
my being in my hands and cannot recognize it:
what sort of creature am I inside of?
Pressing closer to the knowledge
that there is no knowledge, that our world
is visions, shadows, I hear it rumored
that perhaps, who knows, we are living in a cave?

2. Lovers by Sea-Light

the seasons pass by
sunrise noonfall moonset
two lie entwined
tides lap and hiss
at the lips of these bodies
the salt pools
gush overflow or
suck themselves dry
we lie together
as close as shore and sea

3. Call Sign Aquarius

The water I am made of,
free-standing, unencumbered,
has learned to pronounce me and
call me watercourse. Call me:

a hunched and encroaching darkness
ozone clogging the nostrils
a blinding pounce of light
a chuckle of distant thunder
a clod sucking the spatter
and satisfaction of the storm
a pasture glazed with dandelions
and lupines
a bare shouldered sun
in a brisk and clarified sky
songs of a thrush spiralling up
to carol darkness into the drenched woods

In the silence of this white-plastered room,
alone and dry, deranged,
I hum like a transistor with the codes
of faraway weather.

4. *Motley*

Hairband, homespun, opera-hat, afghan,
turtleneck, sheepskin, catskin, buckskin,
denim, dimity, beadwork, braidwork,
rags ripped off from old six-reelers—

all serve as signals to allies and enemies
that Whatintheworld may be taking the air.
Could he be banker, butcher, broker,
madman, marauder, masquerader?

Men who wear ascots, waistcoats, cheviots
are ostracized as doctors, lawyers, palaverers,
rich men and thieves—uncurious costumes!
Young men, beggar men, brawny men saunter

in pigskin, lambskin, desert boots, sandalslippers,
hairshirts and hiphuggers. Others lay footbones
bare to the broken glass, dogshit, chewing gum,
sleep in the park with guitar cases, rucksacks,
stretched on the sidewalk, curbside, fenderwise.

Whether they're indoors, outcast, uptight,
grant them their groin bulges, hairlines, hiplines,
toenails, kneecaps, beardstubble, sticknipples,
grant them their armpits, cockpits, spitballs,
precious possessions, all body-portable.

Better go dogsbody, jackanapes, bareass
than strut through Necropolis unrecognizable,
sexless, seducible, deeply disguisable!

5.   *Into the Future*

Standing here just short of the corner,
I grope with fingertips
against the rasping surface of brick.
If it had handholds I would hang on.
One move could ruin everything.
They would find my blood running down the wall.

In times like these
one never retraces steps. Forward
is the only direction. Beyond this corner
the wind gusts cold, coughing wave-
whirls of dust along Michigan Avenue.
If I let go and turn the corner
what will come at me from my blind side?
A newspaper clutches my leg and forces me on.

6. *Poem of Force*

Sacrifices meant nothing to *me*.
I loved every inch of him: his wrestler's muscles,
his tanks and his missiles naked as mine.
How I kissed his statesman fingers
and his soldier toes!
I tattooed on his breast
the imprint of my body.
Even while sleeping or drunk I guarded
chest, notch, and boundary against his skirmishes.
Never have I understood an ally so well.
He is my darling wolverine.
Keeping him fed full with nourishing rations,
I surmount him like a tower, and he smiles
in gratitude as I draw black blood
from the bodies of his children.

7. *At the Close*

We limp along the shoreline
scuffling and probing for fish
alert enough to eat. Each time
stupefaction chokes us, we stare for breath
out across the sea, abloom
with a jungle of algae.

Birds and hot-breathing beasts are few.
Reptiles have the best of it,
preying on the tumbled bodies
of gulls, on fish that breach
the tangled surface of the sea.
After dark, thallophytes
whisper the truth.

Nights are warmer than formerly.
Everything takes forever—
writing, walking, even stooping,
most of all sleeping.

(I cannot snooze for an hour
without dreaming of drowning.)
At greasy daybreak our faces flush,
and we grow giddy and quarrelsome.

Still, we have more to marvel at
than ever, especially sunsets.
The earth hangs on to air
enough only to breath—none
to make love, none to make war.
The planet hisses with oxygen.

THE OBITUARY WRITER

There are two voices, and the first voice says, "Write!"
And the second voice says, "For whom? . . .
And the first voice says, "For the dead whom thou didst love."
    JOHN BERRYMAN, 1968, QUOTING KIERKEGAARD,
    WHO IN TURN IS QUOTING HAMANN.

When I reach out towards the body of happiness,
a hoarse voice warns me off: "No no. Not *you*."
It must be the obituary writer,
the one who scrambled into print the hour
each poet died, always the first to know.
When off obits. he spoke for Henry, defendant.
He waved goodbye and jumped from a high bridge
and clattered dead on the ice of the Mississippi.
I felt the fall coming all the way to Rome
where I took up pen and paper, an obituary
writer's obituary writer. Quickly death spoke,
shouting in its own hoarse voice. Outside,
across Largo Febo, barely out of eyeshot,
an old mad woman had unmouthed her teeth
to save them for another life. In bib and blanket,
with stockings swathing her ankles, she set her body
adrift from the fourth-floor windowsill. She encountered
the January pavement with a cry.
Soon the *polizia* were snapping photos.
Neighbors huddled together in knots, muttering,
their faces gray as hers. We all mooned over
the swollen object laid out on the cobbles.
The skull was crushed. The flung hands had turned purple.
No one knew her name, least of all the papers.

Dead Henry, better known to all the papers,
was noted alive because, sober, he suffered the shakes.
Drunk, he shrieked and ranted. Who could stand
to stay in the room with him? Not prissy me,
who couldn't abide the hoo-ha, the abasement,
nor my own flinching from his open pain.
His head was full of everybody's death.
His pants sagged, his fly gaped, his hullaballoos

of falling-down drunkenness were an insult to the brain
no matter how hotly and crisply he employed
hangover time for his mettlesome minstrel show
of dreams, obituaries, exhalations.

Some obituary this is: not that of a friend
nor even of an accountant for the fact
of death, of bodies falling alive from heights
in January and landing dead. Admit
that poetry is one of the dangerous trades.
No matter how many we know who have been goaded
by its black promises to deliver
their bodies to the blue snowdrift of death,
it was not poetry, but life, they died of.
Since the day that the old woman took her teeth out
and John the master minstrel turned away
from the gravel of his brother Henry's voice,
there has been no avoiding this obituary.

WALKING THE BOUNDARIES

1. *West, by the Road*

Now swift swallows have flown for the winter.
The last pears have fallen.
Maples, huddled close in the swamp,
slip off their leaves
and lay bare the shaggy cliffwall.
Twigs in damp tangles under
the sagging grasses
abandon themselves to rot,
food for beetles.
Hardiest of their generation, wry apples
clutch at gnarled branches
as long as the wind will let them.

The sumac's crimson seedpods cringe
while the air unleashes the first
fast rangers of milkweed.
under the deep beeches
in leafmold crevices
autumn phalluses
rise up in a single night from
forgotten woodpiles.
The screech of a bluejay batters
naked oak trunks, scattering
bleached goldfinches
wherever they gather on thistles.
The junco's tail flashes
in the cedar. He sings
of two pebbles chipping against one another.

Toppling grasses and unsteady leaves
tolerate the chickadee's scramble
through the drowsy apertures of autumn
toward the house
whose chimney sighs grey woodsmoke
and panes of glass smile earlier each evening.
Roots hunch and contract, their blood runs thin.

They hold forearms
stiff against the wind, while
castaway stones
plunge fistlike for winter
into the ground's gravelled belly.

Sighing, chuckling, the minnow-busy
creek's summer-warm tides,
heartbeat of the sea,
steam and scurry.
The thatch of the marsh holds hard:
it crouches down on matted fibers
to quake at air but yield its seed to water.
Come January, grumbling glaciers
will walk uphill in the arms
of northeast gales to shear
a year's marsh hay
and macerate against the granite
piers of the bridge
the buried shells of snails.

Moles burrow down to the frostline.
Starlings hang on in holes
hard-won from woodpeckers.
Squirrels, walled up between
skyscrapers of hickory nuts (all
stolen except for a handful
of windfalls wrapped in their husks)
duck down under the barn.

Snow is coming. Snow
is coming. All but birds
will be buried. Water will
absent itself till spring,
while earth locks up into its mineral meaning.
Only yesterday we breathed a world
of liquor and seed. It hardens now.
The little animals lie panting,
sleepless, winterless,
anticipating drift and flake,
awaiting the crackle of frozen meat

upon the tongue. Their lungs
bloom like flowers
at the alienation of the air.

2.   *South, by the Wall*

The trees are choiring their light at the house.
A new-minted copper beech stands burnished
at its greening sister's side
crying aloud with the zeal of its leaves,
which have unfolded this morning like lemur's
fingers. In the swamp, ferns uncurl
their bedsprings. The meadow grass,
as thick as fur, crowds on itself
to gobble up yesterday's rain.

No passageway is left in the pasture
for large-footed beasts, only room for speckled
clutches of eggs and the tender claws
of new-hatched fawn-spotted pheasant,
hiding and scuttling between the scented
trunks of grass-stalk and grass-stalk.
Spiderwebs balloon with bubbles of dew
while their mistresses stopple their breathing-tubes,
travelling upward and down,
inching and testing.

As soon as the sun has ripened
toward the hammered gold of sunset,
it departs for its nightly reception
in the West, leaving the sky all pearls.
Mice and moles, peepers and woodcock,
speak up in twittering singsongs.
Robins yodel. Owls and night-herons
scream and crawk.

Out of sight of the sun the plants
lie quiet. They snuff their inner candles

as the moon combs through fledgling trees
to ruffle the landscape and frost their leaves
with the filigree of moonshine.
This is the time for sleep.
We will feed even better tomorrow, and after
the sun mounts high, breed till our brains burst
with the bluebell music of flickers and grackles.

3.   *East, by the Cliff*

The pasture, freckled with patches
of elderly snow, flutters pale flags
of martyred goldenrod. Ice pokes and clutches
into the female cleft of the Indian rock.
From high vantage in our eldest hickory
jays engage in an antiphony
of creditable outrage
against their rivals the crows
who station themselves in the maples.

My breath is glue in my nostrils.
Mere air holds the sleeping marsh
solidly in chains, it crumples
the recent thaw's ruts
into hogback ridges
that the sun when it waxes
will take much trouble
to melt down again
into March mud.

Barren as an unlocated satellite,
this moment is dustless and rigid.
Only the gurgle and scurry
of blood-salt tides can
irrigate these badlands,
scatter the ice-floes, patiently flush
the mud-bottomed creeks, never mind remorse,
into the patiently receptive sea.

The barking of bored dogs
rattles the hard hillside.
The jays protest, chickadees chatter,
fierce finches whimper.
Pent and braggart geese
in my neighbor's corral
cackle echoes against
my iced-over windowpanes.

Our beechwoods have given up
their ghosts to mushrooms.
Plumes from grosgrain chimneys
remind me with woodsmoke
how, crisply thrusting and stretching,
roots and bowed branches conveyed
quick currents of sap
through the longtime noontimes
of longago summers.

A pewter-colored sky
tightens up into zinc
as the momentary day flickers
toward sundown. Breath from the South
drops heathery hints of a promise,
but the North rides back in its tracks
at the near edge of dark to retract it.

This is the season of waiting for light,
of electric nights, of unrecognized footprints.
Wan woodpiles and slumbering straw
nurse reliquaries of calories
against the scorch of wind and the hiss of snow.
They sing lullabies across the chasm
between this dangerous land
and the whispering sun.

4. The Woodcock

Inside my human walls I sit surrounded
by scurrying music. Voices sing *Kyrie*.
My eyesight ranges out across the field.
Those acres tolerate us as their maker does,
suffering denials without a sound,
courtesies and rain without a smile.
They've settled for the edge of land and sea.
Downstream, northerly, the restless waters
search up the creek twice every day
and twice a day back off to leave it dry.
At certain tides the place has the look of an island;
at others, a desert of cold mud. Crops germinate
to feed the appetites of muskrat and mackerel.
This is saltmarsh country, two-way country,
no-man's land for gill beasts and lung beasts.
Its frontiers meander, liquefied, unmeasured.

Color fades out of the field as though the sun
had dipped into the earth to stain the clouds.
Indoors the singers climb the scale from mercy
to glory, from belief past blessing to
a resolution—the unimaginable plea
that a Lamb should Grant us Peace—and then are silent.
Over the land and sea, air cools and hardens.
A thrush sings its Goodnight. Among the maples
of the swamp, peepers fiddle their shrill chorus,
toads who have somewhere learned to sing like birds.
Here, where coastline edges off the forest
and the woodland's freshet leavings leak away
to modify the high tide's appetite,
I hear the woodcock's sundown declaration
that he too is ready to sing. There's light enough
left for me to see the dumpy body
as it shuffles among the tufts of last year's grass,
restless and ready for nightflight. Hear the blare
of his tiny trumpet, so sharp a sound that he
must hunch his shoulders to squeeze it out. Again

and again his music sends the lively word
to the edge of the woods and out across the marsh
as though this Orpheus could command his voice
to travel back and forth between the worlds
just as his wondrous delicate bill can probe
the soggy earth for worms.
                              Now we have arrived
at the edge of darkness, and the woodcock, darkened,
leaps aloft with a whirr of wings. Wings?
No, music—his voice, he is singing! He rises up
past the dark treetops to the graying sky.
As he leaves the earth his song ascends
higher and higher, pitch upon pitch, spiral
after spiral. At last, at the top of his helix
three hundred feet or more, it is enough,
he can rise no farther on the updraft of this song,
he has reached a boundary. He starts to fall,
he topples from the peak, repulsed by sky,
he dips zigzag and loops and twitters earthward,
his song hot on the wingbeats of his flight,
coiling in chirrups of retreating tailspin.
Plunge and flutter. Silence. He glides
from the edge of light across the edge of dark
to alight upon the very shadowed patch
of earth from which the night had lifted him.
A pause for breath. He trumpets out a warning
that *this* was not a failure. He collects
himself to ascend again, to reach beyond
the edge of the habitable world, beyond
his limits of heaviness and incarnation.

Gills dried up long since, useless on land.
Fins flowered into three-toed featherweight
tuckaway talons for pouncing and perching.
The brain, too massive to fly very far with,
dwindled in birds once flippers became wings
and danger need no longer be outwitted
but merely flown away from, left behind.
How much is left behind at boundaries!
Arising from the sea we lost our lightness.
Thought took us to the woods, where vision blurred,

for sight and mind do not take wing together.
Body at least is bound within a landscape,
an earth that holds us fastened to the seasons
for food and footing, birth and burial.
Regardless of the gifts we've left behind
and all the boundaries we cannot cross,
some power lets us press beyond our powers:
echoes of wind, of ebb and flow, of heartbeat,
singing that trickles landward with the waters,
music that clambers skyward through the dark.

STANDING FAST: FOX INTO HEDGEHOG

After these years of sniffing the air at hedges,
leaping so gingerly as to leave no footprints,
tiptoeing through streams to wash off my own scent,
and walking welcome at night into the houses of hens,
my paws grow clumsy; my spine curls into a hoop;
these claws must be given over to scrabbling and scuttling.

No more prancing. My snout, the air-taster,
now stiffens itself for rooting. The silken ears,
the blazing trail, the shimmering pelt, gather up
the color of gray earth. No more flight or pursuit.

Quarry for all comers, I crouch in furrows,
keep away from light, bristle at a footfall,
my body set up for surprise. Stand fast, here, now.
No call to run quick. I know what I know.

GROUND

This stuff is what we are born from. Before my eyes
and between my fingers—grainy, sticky, chalky—
the provisions lie at hand for life to burst out of.
How stubbornly it behaves, baked hard as biscuits
in summer, yet, thawed by spring, spreading wide
to swallow a hundred horses, and in winter
rigid enough to scrape knuckles and crack bones.
It would seem to yield no passage, except that roots
as delicate as hairs can pierce hardscrabble
without a bruise or blister and hold their course
whether opposed by gravel or mud. By tasting it,
farmers can guess at what may come of its favors,
whether their crops will require manure or limestone.
We savor in the first-plucked leaf of lettuce
the lingering fragrance of Sun, which slips away
with the soil that bestowed it almost within the hour,
just as fish lose their colors out of water . . .
as I would despair if you were dead.

DARK HOUSES

For Edward Davison (1970–1898)

> *I shall come back at last,*
> *In this dark house to die.*
> EDWARD DAVISON, 1919

1. *At Seventy-One. New York.*

Words have finally failed this balloon of a body,
White as a side of bacon, cold as the plank
It heightens like foothills under a sheet in the morgue.
Inside it, living, smoldered poetry
Like January wasps that stir in summer houses.
Parched past a trickle now, his will had wrestled
Headlong through the pastures of his youth
In floods of love. He squandered it, spent it on girls
Who took his rings and sold them for a ribbon,
Leaving him petulance and loyalty
As stones in drought, no longer bathed by love.
In spite of years and years of wearing down,
The words whose slave he was could still surprise him.
Lying half-blind, his lips alive with poems,
In his delirium his voice cried out again
With "Elsie Marley", "The Tyger", "O Mistress Mine",
'Led by a blind and teachit by a bairn'.
From the first breath in Glasgow to the last
Shudder in Mount Sinai Hospital,
Words, and the songs of words, convinced his life.
No words go walking in a darkened house.

2. *At Fifty. Pennsylvania.*

His days of life grew drier with the years
Or dwindled into place-names on a map.
In his own eyes, what cracks across the glass,
Betrayals he had given and received?

Lord, I am not worthy to sit at Thy table.
He downed each whisky like a punishment
To keep his heart from thumping with the shame
Of memory and waste. 'The parable of the talents
Lies on my conscience like a heavy weight.'
Buried was the hate of his treacherous father
In old men whom he loved. He worked to win,
And won, their praise, as heavy as a father's,
But praise from such could never quite be trusted.
Buried, buried were all his loves and flowers
In the woman who never calmed him but inflamed
His anger. O buried deep inside inside
But bursting out in coughs that stretched and tore
His chest and neck in the tempest of his rage,
Dry places racked him with a daily taste
Of all that wrestles poetry to earth.

3.   *At Forty. Colorado.*

Hard by these mountains, cottonwoods and creeks,
He pitched his camp, the woman at his side,
And basked in the dry light of his latest father—
President, chief scholar, neighbor, friend.
The world of London letters grew more faint,
But students clustered round. His voice, reciting,
Drew them to poetry as to a mass.
What he saw kindled in their faces helped
Him hope for recompense from poetry,
For poetry is what he spent for them.
She would not wind her arms around his arms
Nor would he cleave to her, forsaking others.
Exiled, admired, content and yet dismayed,
He came into his own as son and father
Just as he, knowingly, went down as poet.
Without the nourishment of loneliness
Or lovers to betray him, poetry
Turned from his bed, his page, but not his life.
Desertion is not charged in this affair.

4. *At Thirty. On Tour.*

His heart's love now laid bare, he gives pursuit
Across an ocean, putting her to proof.
She flies before him, hesitates, surrenders,
But only for the moment. He must set
His mark on her, let her not disappear,
For she will never answer all his letters.
Sinking his past behind him, he embarks
On the *Britannic Sea* and lands, surprised,
At Montreal to garner his reward.
In wilderness, beside the Rangeley Lakes,
Amid the barbershops and alien corn,
He finds her. Is it he she's waiting for?
Her eyes more than her voice confess she's true.
Scanning a whole new continent for the prize
He values most, the treasure that eludes him,
He searches eagerly as ever for
The faithful woman, the approving elder,
And finds his heart's desire, as we all do:
A wife, a chief; a mother and a father.
Prizes are given him, but he must strive
To test them countless times for certainty,
For assay. Can it be true? Can it be true?
Poems have promised him it would be true.

5. *At Twenty-Two. Cambridge.*

His Cambridge was the Cambridge of the poets—
Dawn on the river, fervency of friendship,
Young men striving. (Dream no more of dark houses.)
His editor and benefactor, Squire,
Cool as a father in his patronage,
Lent almost every pound he could afford
Whenever he remembered to enclose it.
Spurred on, the student edited, disputed,
Wrangled and charmed. ('Breakfast with Sidney Webb.'
'Sassoon and Arnold Bennett came to tea.')
He drenched himself in poetry that held
To English tunes. His poems sprang to paper

And into print. He grieved and swore and counted
The ways his love betrayed him, while his friends,
Ackerley, Kitto, Priestley, Campbell, Kendon,
Bound by the lavish loyalties of youth,
Stood by his midnights, heard out his laments,
Read him their poems in return for his.
He was, it was said, the perfect Cambridge poet.
No one at Cambridge carried so much poetry
Close to the surface, fresh and potable.
Sluicing and plunging through a hundred months
Of loves and labors, quarrels, debts and rages,
He squandered all the energy (he mourned
In later years) that should have served to carry
His poems out of luck and into truth.
After so ravening an orgy, fear
Of weariness would trouble him forever.

6. *At Sixteen. South Shields.*

His mother sits alone in the narrow house
On a Tyneside street, waiting for the weekly
Cheque to arrive from the man the children knew
As Uncle Ted. The weeks it did not come
The milkman and the grocer gave her credit
Because she always spoke to them like a lady.
When did the boy first hear the sound of poems?
Not in the slums, the collieries and streets
Where draymen, coalmen, dustmen clumped and ranted.
Not in the South Shields Empire Theatre where jugglers,
Comics and pratfall people woke the dead
At ten performances a week while he
Sat in the darkness of the street outside,
A ticket-seller at fifteen. The following year
(Six inches yet to grow till he was grown)
He called himself eighteen and sought his fortune,
A place in Churchill's Royal Naval Division,
Setting to work on his self-education.
He sat in uniform and did the duty
For five years keeping records at the Crystal Palace.
Poetry came to him, beginning with Sophocles,

Tennyson (Everyman Library), Spenser, Shakespeare,
Lamb and Coleridge. Behind them all lay
The Church of England, where still the language of Cranmer
Rang like a bell. Lord, I am not worthy to sit at Thy table.
And, seasoning this, 'Woman, her power and charm'.

7.　*His Rest, 1970. Massachusetts.*

Now life has blunted the edges of his fury.
Mistrals of laceration and self-betrayal
Wither his bloom, bring frost to the harvest of youth.
His childhood, trodden beneath an implacable boot,
Lies motionless as memory in water
Where bones lie scattered shellmeal on the bottom.
Stricken by years of labor and rancor, all
For little but a blessing by the fathers,
The poet dies. A creature dies with him
Who had long lost the way into his poems.
We never understood his shrieks of rage
Damning the multitude of mousy deaths
That, year by year, would parch him into silence—
A swollen body lying on a plank.
Surviving him, we carry the poet's flesh
Reduced to ashes in a canister
Along a path to the summit of a cliff
Where Indians used to hold their summer vigil
Over the shellfish marshes and the sea.
We let the bones and ashes tumble out,
Dusting the granite in their heavy fall
Until they catch and rest in crevices
Or sink dissolving in the tepid brack
Of marsh below. And now his thirsty body
Is part of the land at last, land of his children,
Where the gray ungiving stone can always stand
For fathers, thrusting up above the fields
Not ever his own, though dearer than the land
That gave him birth but never knew his name.

FROM

PRETENDING TO BE ASLEEP

(*1970*)

STUMPS

The field is studded with their thousand lives.
All that is left of all that tracery
Pokes through the goldenrod in amputations
Too short to see, too tall to be mown over.
Their knuckles sprout new fingers every April.
I go my rounds in August trimming them back.
The roots, now elderly, are just as far
Involved in growing as they ever were,
But their suckers are sickly and cannot survive
Unless they're given help by God or me.

After a year or two of this flirtation
I snap trees off by hand which saw and axe
Once needed all their edges to bring down.
Reason could lull these lives to a merciful end,
But I as owner claim the dark indulgence
Of giving them a chance to sprout once more.
Crops like mine are not so much planted as buried.

IN THE SIXTIES

1. *The Pleaders*

What are you going to do with us, who have
No edges, no talents, no discriminations,
Who hear no inner voices, who perceive
No visions of the future, no horizons?
We are among you; we are going to stay.

We crush, we drag, we heave, we draw the water
For you to spill. We gather together to listen
To your speeches, though your tongues run on so fast
We cannot follow, and your jokes dart in and out
Too quickly for our laughter to form itself.
We are your children, whom you treat like horses.

When crowds surge out into the streets
You have invited them; we run with them.
You give us order, speak on our behalf,
For we speak up too slowly to interrupt you.
We are the numbers ranked on your computers.
We are among you; we are going to stay.

If we knew how to pray to you, we'd pray
That you could listen long enough to listen
To what it is we think we want. We know
That what you think we want lies far away
From anything that has occurred to us.
We are your children, whom you treat like horses.

We are the eyes your eyes have never met.
We are the voice you will not wait to hear.
We are the part of you you have forgotten,
Or trampled out, or lost and wept to lose.
We are your children, whom you treat like horses.
We are among you; we are going to stay.

2. *The Gun Hand*

You have been looking out for me. I held
A pistol to the ear of the Saigon captive.
It's been a busy year. I plugged the preacher
As he leaned on the lattice railing of his motel
And drilled the senator as he strode among the busboys.
I have aimed a thousand killers of all calibres
At television pictures, egg-hatted cops,
At the pulsing cartilage of a child's temple,
At the upstart cars that pass mine on the right.
I have squeezed so often you might think me weary,
But my hand is poised and clenched to squeeze again
At the next target of opportunity.

3. *What Counts*

Our astronomic signallers are sure
That what they send is monitored Out There.
Whether the creatures who receive Earth's signals
Wear flesh or bone or neither, the reply
We get will be conveyed to us in numbers,
So those who man this world must be prepared
For grammar with no language. (A pulse, we call
Such signals? But that stands for blood with us.)

The words we use to amplify our numbers
Will count for little. Though they 'see the stars',
Our far communicants can send us nothing
That we have any names for—only numbers
Which in space-dialogue refer to nothing,
Not food or love, but only to themselves.
It could be heart alone that counts out there,
But without language we shall never know.

For days the television seared our eyes
with images of the many-widowed family.
We crouched to stare at their loosened faces, their fingers
on rosaries, the hunched and harnessed shoulders.
(We starve for what survival has to teach us.)
Term after term their champions had been chosen,
served, shot down, reciting Aeschylus
and Tennyson. (" 'Tis not too late to seek
a newer world," and other familiar quotations.)

Too late, as usual, the latest killing
instructs us in our love for those who seek
more than we think of seeking. Soft in our seats
we watch the people of the long procession
reeling out across the summer landscape
to hide a body shredded and cold with bullets.
No one can hold his tongue: shrilled editorials,
New Year's resolutions, blurted promises
drown out the inner yelp of unmastered hounds
who press and snuffle hungrily along
the course this body leads us. At last, at night,
his remnants vanish in the grainy ground.

Before and after death we coursed that body.
No matter if words attacked, we could shrug them off,
but his image aroused our desire and nudged our hatred.
Slogging up mountains, seized by rapids, breasting
breakers, standing stripped naked by crowds,
his body sexed us. It revealed a self
our mirrors had never included. Gawky, controlled,
athletic in action, hectoring in speech,
it performed deeds that could have broken us
and left us with the trophies of last year's hunting—
whistles, grunts, imitated animals.

'Change,' his body said—but when we heard
our voices speaking, they were not our voices.
His body has emptied the screens of our sight.
The people are not listening to voices.

5. *The Two of You*

I

Your face is tense as wire within a wire
    When you consent to bed with sunlight flying.
The dervish flashes up into the fire.
    Not to be lost to love is to be dying.

Molten and greedy, quivering in my arms,
    You gnaw, you tear, you moan beneath my prying.
Our veins are full of sunlight as a field.
    Not to be lost to love is to be dying.

These fearful bodies rage against our will—
    Our love is truth and leaves no room for lying.
These stones, these walls, this house, this windowsill
    Are not to be lost. To love is to be dying.

II

Outdoors the breeze blows childlike, notwithstanding
    Tomorrow it could be carrying sounds of war.
As we pass, we turn toward each other,
    Lovers in a bed.

We preserve house-plants, growing creatures,
    By constancy of warmth. In their season
Light airs are given entrance. We exclude only
    The brazen airs that turn flesh into stone.

Nourished by our senses and attentions
    This house will open up into a palace
Where children dress themselves in royal robes
    And swagger with the certainty of angels.

To hear one another's voices without speaking
    Makes up the music of this house. The time
Of storms is welcomed as a penance.
    This house is silent and fragile as God.

6.   *A Word in Your Ear on Behalf of Indifference*

History is sometimes salvaged by it, a civil servant
Who bows and smiles at weakness, at right and wrong;
At progress, poverty, peace and war; at victims,
Torture, and torturers. A skilled masseur,
Indifference smooths our faces into features
And lets our muscles work without rending each other.

Indifference-in-the-home lets tiring lovers
Share a warm bed between the defloration and
The signal for the soon-to-be-contested
Divorce to plunge both parties
In ice-water up to the arse.

Though we yell back and forth, 'Let us erase our existence!'
'Let us scurry before the flailing winds of our senses!'
'Let us surrender into the hands of the forces!'
Indifference chimes in to discourage us from jumping.

My client gives us the power this side of death
To shackle ourselves, to live within our dimensions,
To ignore for hours at a time
The outrage and the dread
Of being no more than we are.

THE LOSING STRUGGLE

A Chinese word for landscape is made up of two
characters meaning "mountains" and "waters."
ROSS TERRILL: *800,000,000*

To yield words easily gives pleasure
To the tongue that speeds their flow,
But, loosed, they linger on the surface
Like unexpected, unpenetrating rain.

Where are we to seek the words for life?
And how are we to see what must be seen
Before shaping our language to the sound of it?
What must be seen is every moment present

But hardly every moment seen. What I hear,
Like the muttering of a crowd, is seldom discerned
Although the murmur is never interrupted.
My body secretes against its rarest need.

When released, by lightning or alarum,
I can run like a deer, ravage like a lion, overhear
The creak of a mouse's toe on a wisp of straw.
Except for these times I sleep.

What are the repositories in myself
That bind me in the caverns of silence
And refuse to let me ramble at my will?
My ego stamps its foot at their refusal.

By the shore the sun embraces me.
The pleasures of water ripple through me
And take me by the singing throat.
The elms across the lake shine out like torches.

By another shore I watch the ocean scurry
Over its deeps of flounder and periwinkles,
Bearing its rockweed aloft like torches.
As its tide falls and the sandbar emerges, birds alight.

Here by the sea I cannot see as far as the mountains,
Nor do they loom over my shoulder as they once did.
Change is everything here, here everything changes,
Changes with the phases of the moon.

I have come to worship the sun, clouds, clarity,
And as deeply I distrust the moon.
I cannot bear the monthly flow of blood.
Tide and change corrupt the imagination.

I spin my fancies finer and finer,
A quota of gossamer every working day
From an old spider who does not care for flies
And webs it for the sake of the design.

My name is death. I freeze the world in light.
I see my arm, poised at my side to move,
But never moving; and my eye, my eye
Is fixed on what exists beyond existence.

OLD PHOTOGRAPH

Eight years dead, and dying
Many months before that, you leave me
No trace of yourself, except
These yellowing prints and some letters.
What do we know of the dead?
The needle of memory scratches
In the effort to remember.

Everything has been taken care of,
The papers are filed,
Most of the photographs mislaid
In a cigar-box.
Only this propped-up pose remains,
Rigid on the piano in pious memory.

While you were dying I shuddered
At every jolt of pain that shot through you,
Watched as you speechlessly
Contorted with a numb tongue
To speak of your dying.
I was told I would forget that
And retain the memory of you
In the sounds of your husky laughter,
Your charm in company,
The glee you took in never
Saying Goodbye on the telephone.

It isn't true. "True feeling
Leaves no memory," as Stendhal said.
It has left me nothing of you
But reminders that remind me of nothing.
Besides, only grief, sleeplessness,
Infant despair, betrayal.
These are you. I know nothing else
About you any more. I live behind glass,
Framed as tightly as your picture,

As frozen, as rigid, as blind.
How can I keep in touch
When there is nothing to touch?

23 September 1967

THE LAST WORD

When I saw your head bow, I knew I had beaten you.
You shed no tears—not near me—but held your neck
Bare for the blow I had been too frightened
Ever to deliver, even in words. And now,
In spite of me, plummeting it came.
Frozen we both waited for its fall.

Most of what you gave me I have forgotten
With my mind but taken into my body,
But this I remember well: the bones of your neck
And the strain in my shoulders as I heaved up that huge
Double blade and snapped my wrists to swing
The handle down and heard the axe's edge
Nick through your flesh and creak into the block.

AFTER BEING AWAY

When I shall die, in body
or mind, if you survive me,
give me my due. You know
I held no certain magic
and threw no light before me.
Searching out of pain
at first, then out of habit,
and out of self at last,
I stumbled on surprises
and managed to record them.
There's only one surprise—
to be alive—and that
may be forgotten daily
if daily not remembered.
Sometimes I remembered it.

You too, my love, have watched
each day for its surprises
and touched them as they happened.
Forgive me for inflicting
my pride on your surprises
and holding to the few
that were my sole possession.

Surprise we had together
in afternoon or evening
when we were close together
or even, often, parted.
I thank you for the thousand
surprises that you gave me,
not least the gift, unhinted
and endlessly surprising,
of never being absent.

PRETENDING TO BE ASLEEP

If a man could pass through Paradise in a dream,
and have a flower presented to him as a pledge that his
soul had really been there, and if he found that flower
in his hand when he awoke—Ay!—and what then?
                    COLERIDGE: *Anima Poetae*

1. *The Deserted Poet*

This part of the country is underpeopled.
Not a word waits in hiding under the ferns
To reach up for my hand and lead me out
Of myself. No words have passed this way this season:
I have forgotten even the sound of their footsteps
Whickering through the leaves at my approach.

Look at my face, never an honest one.
It covers my desertion by pretending
That words have never meant a thing to me.
This face settles for the lie. It puts on
Creases of feigned anger between the eyes,
Furrows of mock surprise across the brow.

I wear the mask of an actor who returns
From a long journey to find his wife and children dead.

2. *In the Dock*

Tried by the day, I stand condemned at night.
The evidence of years of fraud and shame
Waits until darkness to be brought to light.
Crime hangs from every letter of my name.

Each day conceals its treachery and blight
In places no defendant could disclaim:
Beneath the shirt, the mattress, out of sight
Behind the portrait smiling from its frame.

Night comes to sentence me. My second sight
Fixes me steadily within its aim
And squeezes slowly. With a shriek of fright
I fall forever from the cliffs of blame.

Watching my body vanish, I awake
To hear the sounds I never thought to make.

3. *Under Protection*

One side wet and one side dry,
My skin walls out the world.
I am blockaded, only barely in touch.
Life stiffens and keeps its distance.

I coast in tides of light and cold
Past knife-edge noises and the smoke of cities.
The daily lives that shoulder the sound of my name
Seethe distantly across the flats of time.

I have dreamed myself into the streets
Of a village on market day. Aloft on the battlements
I command the town and prepare to seize
The contraband bartered by peddlers.

Boots dazzling, muscles like halyards,
My subordinates stand tiptoe in their barrack,
Braced at unblinking armed attention
For the clang of the summons to suppress disorder.

Out there the life could be just anyone's,
But it happens to be mine.
And do I govern it, pay taxes on it?
No, it is mine, but it offers me no friendship.
It surrounds me.

4. *The Flower of Sleep*

When danger strips the mind
And slithers toward my throat,
I slink away in hopes to stay
Alive, aloft, afloat.

I cringe from the land of light
To bury myself in sleep
As though a sea surrounded me
Of endless dark and deep.

There dreamers hand me flowers,
Presuming me to be dead.
'No reason why he'd choose to lie
Asleep in a death-bed.'

In this cradle of desperate rest
I snore away all fear—
The toppling tree, the storm at sea,
The Goddess striding near.

Such sleep does more than dream,
For when the sounds of day
Bring life to sight, I welcome light
To shudder my fear away.

But lately I dream of sleep,
Of wrecks and falling trees,
Of flowers laced around my waist
And grappling at my knees.

5. *The Public Garden*

I.
This public park and I are strangers.
Look at it; sit on its benches; no matter.
It sleeps though I am agog in its presence.

My turn to sleep. The park enters my privacy.
It wakes trembling in the spaces of my skull.
Its dry bones burst, its benches are my lovers.

III

Each day the avenues I roam at night
Shut down when I awake, and no pretense
Of sleep will penetrate their spaces.
The visiting hours are over in the garden.

6.   *The Visitant*

You make yourself known to me in surprising places:
A laundry or a bus, or late at my office desk
After the others have gone, or where I listen
To an unspoiled voice read out a familiar poem.

Distracted, clouded over, I am startled
Awake by your presence stealing up behind me
To draw my breath and raise your hands and clasp
The soft familiar palms over my eyes.

7.   *Pretending to be Awake*

I am disgusted by the earthworks of my protection.
The clothes stink that curtain my nakedness,
And beneath the wool my flesh is beginning to fester.
I must tease my life awake that now lies sleeping.

Others stay awake in the dark by laceration,
By thrashing out at workers, lovers, children,
To keep their ears alert to the sound of sorrow.

Some plunge into the tolerance of women
Or paralyze the tendrils of their brains
Desiring visions beyond sleep or waking.

If I could tempt this sleeping life awake!
It shuns me now that sometime did me seek.

8.   *The Cost of Pretending*

I would despise myself if I had the strength for it,
Would welcome the knife slitting the skin of my neck
As long as it did not falter and pour the blood.
Give me your hand, put it beneath my arm
Which closes on it, next to my heart. What
Do you hear of me? A steady beat, dull, leaden,
Irreversible. One who survives everything
Will shortly survive even himself.

9.   *The Voices*

I know those voices. They are all mine.
Tuesday the infant,
Wednesday the child,
Thursday the grown man wheedling
In rut or yearning in prayer,
Friday the sexless ancient, dreaming of sex.

Through the country of sleep
The voice of my blood
Trickles like water over limestone ledges.
Tributaries borrow its *bel canto*
To stage-whisper their way through dreams
Or heroize the arias of nightmare.

The voice is me, whatever voice or stream,
The voice of history rising through my sources.

10. *First Voice: The Child*

Strange feet upon the stairs
Turn and walk this way.
I clothe myself in sleep
By shutting off my light.
They will not find the scent
Of hate on me tonight.

With one huge sigh, my chest
Moves easy, at the rate
Of every thief who breathes
More slowly than his guilt.
The door creaks open, but
My face, disguised in sleep,
Sings children's choruses.

The door has shut. The steps
Give way, descend the stairs.
The light, the book, emerge
From hiding. Like a bear
In blankets, all alert
For footsteps to ascend,
I lurk here in my lair.
They come? Then I'll pretend
Again to be asleep.

11. *Second Voice: The Youth*

What wakened me? Moon?
Rustle of willows?
A cry or creaking stair?
Or was it shadows
Troubling my sleep
With a tug at my pillows?

Out of the shadows
Where sleep had been hiding
An ominous parcel
Comes quietly sliding—
Charred bones and ashes
On the tide riding.

Who could the parent be
Of this delivery?
Hands cold as serpents
Fumble the frippery,
Wrench at the wrapping,
Pause and lie quivering.

No, let it lie there
Inside its adorning.
Now should I stand to arms
After such warning,
Or pace the aisles of night
Until morning?

12.   *Third Voice: The Widower*

The world has spread the word
That I am unworthy of it,
Crouching in lairs and caves
Pretending to be asleep.

First of the warnings: Love
Opened her eyes to me,
Then stopped her breath. No more
Pretending to be asleep.

Next came attentions, lavished
By divorcees and widows.
Though I took their bodies, mine
Pretended to be asleep.

Then came the nights, each darker
Than the one before. By night
I had no part to play.
By day I seemed asleep.

I know the sun by name.
This darkness may give ground
If I dream my way awake,
Pretending to be asleep.

13.   *Fourth Voice: The Grandmother*

I am an old woman living in a house beset with men.
It has been years since I heard a child
singing to itself.

These little men of mine are so little mine.
They live in the same dwelling but at a terrible distance.
They bring me their flowers but never notice me.
They wrestle with themselves,
with each other, father and son,
at all hours. I carry them platters of food.
They eat. They think themselves to be alone.
They walk like crustaceans.

There is no way for me to say, 'Awake.'
I must go on forever, smiling, serving, alert
for the accident of their waking.

Once young men stirred out of sleep
and smiled to find me naked beside them.
They gave me the flower of themselves,
the flower of their dream.
My little men do not yet know
they have been presented flowers.
They cannot recognize the face of the beloved
in their dream. How can they know,
unless they wake, that they have only
been pretending to be asleep?

14. *Possession*

Inside me lives someone who writes poems,
Someone who has no words but from time to time
Borrows my words, whirls them through the dance
Of his purposes, then returns them.

My only evidence for his existence
Comes when I find poems on my desk
Ready for me to revise.
                              When did this happen?

Though I have never known who scribbled them
In secret, still I know my job.
I find them ready and waiting, I take over.
Possession they say is nine points in the poem.

MAKING MARKS

No two conventions of teeth behave alike.
Some chatter, grip, or slash. Others strike.
Thirty-two counters measure out our breath.
What other course for words but past the teeth?
The human body holds them at its height
Better to speak with, but the worse to bite.

Teeth hold the resonance for speech and song,
Which cannot rise past tunelessness for long
Unless teeth govern them to soar and lilt—
To pierce with love or hate up to the hilt.
Smiling, though soft in cheek, is hard in bone,
And sounds make words by trickling over stone
To give the tongue an edge to call its own.

Sounds are the stuff, yet letters are the knives
In each man's voice, the shape of what survives.
Dry bones alone can live, though fossilized
Forever. Let my words be recognized
As mine by the wear of their bite. They classify
The being that they once were brandished by
And the abrasives they were sharpened with.
This way he gnawed his life and grinned his death.

FROM

THE CITY AND THE ISLAND

(*1966*)

THE COLLECTOR

How the meadows dazzle this morning!
Every songbird's throat is gasping
To swallow deeper draughts of sunlight.
The fresh flowers gape as thirsty as the birds.

Like the web of a net my path crisscrosses
The piebald fields from wood to marsh
On the trail of plump lady slipper
Or openhearted blackeyed susan.

They flee me—lupine, arbutus, arethusa,
Dawn flowers fresh as the birds' dawn song—
Yet I am patient. There will be others.
Journeys end in lovers meeting.

Another day, another conquest:
The blush in the shadows, the crisp stem,
The velvet flesh against my fingers,
Head drooped prettily against my chest.

Hardly a field without its encounter!
Here are my prizes; here again, flowers
Taken in unlikely places and postures.
Some time I could tell you stories.

As the years pass, I take greater pleasure
In boasting where I found heart's-ease,
Forget-me-not, all the pretty creatures
That yearned so ardently from their dewy beds.

GIFTS

When I was a child, a heartstruck neighbor died
On her birthday. Dying was strange enough,
But what a way to choose to spend your birthday,
I thought, and what sort of a gift was this?
From time to time, people have done it since—
Dying in the environs of a celebration
As though they had picked out the day themselves.
Perhaps they had, one way or another,
Prayed for something to happen, and prayed wrong.
Sophocles, when old enough to die,
Suspected prayer and entered a caveat:
'Zeus, act kindly whether or not I pray;
And, though I plead for it, turn harm away.'
I keep a wary silence on my birthdays,
Make up no lists at Christmas, lie low
When asked what I *really* want. How should I know?
Best ask for gifts as though I had none coming.

THE CITY AND THE ISLAND

1. *For Amphibians*

I say my goodbyes
To orange peels, eggshells,
Chicken guts, celery,
Row a stroke homeward,
Then wait for gulls
To pick the stuff over.
Gulls are getting choosier
Here in the tideway,
But the sea never stops
Gulping and nibbling.

Bottles, bravest
Of all the garbage
I scuttle offshore,
End up mumbled
Down among the lobsters.
Tides or a loop of line
Sometimes unwater them:
What was clear, clouded,
Messages faded,
Contents doubtful.

Landsmen like me
Are shocked when sailors
Turn to the sea
As the place to retire
Whatever's unwanted
From soup to cadavers;
Yet they draw on its water
For all but libation
And bite without fear
Into fish that have eaten
Whatever we feed them.

The sun sinks down,
Crossed by a cormorant
Hastening homeward.
I turn to the oars
And row myself out of it,
Make my skiff fast,
Stamp feet on shore,
My pail rinsed clean
Of provisions, garbage,
Salt water, all.

To walk the path landward
I turn my back seaward.

2. *Song: Bright Being*

Past the rich meadowland of the senses
Shade mingles and stirs in the clearings.
In that island where oranges blossom
    I seek you, child, again.

On the shore where surf scurries hissing
And the sand scrapes under your shoulder,
Where tides nuzzle sweetly together,
    I hold you, child, again.

In the heat of wet tongues and embraces,
In the shuddering bed where Love
Can never quite be requited,
    I lie with you again.

That childhood has lasted forever
In a forest of tottering archways.
Sink down in the echoing moonlight
    And die with me again.

3. *The Emigration: Newfoundland 1965*

Love, there are reasons why I must be free
> To put to sea.
> No matter how the body aches
To keep in touch, touch has its failures too.
The mind is helped to heal by travelling,
> And so I offer to the wake's
> Brutal unravelling
The old perplexities of course and crew.

My dream has never changed: abandoned far
> From shore I float
> Aboard an ill-found boat
Unhelped by oar or sail, landfall or star
To guide by. Currents jostle me at will.
> The wallowing shallop makes her way
> Through the long day.
I cannot steer; I must not let her fill.

Halfway between the city and the island I
> Am bound for the city.
> The island had its terrifying
Pastures. There the bones of strangers lie
Unburied where we slew them without pity.
> We watched them, dead and dying,
> In the long light
And hugged the memory for many a night.

In flight from the unspeakable, we float
> Our household in a boat,
> Leaving behind us every grave
Of every ancestor we can recall.
The family mountains fade over our stern.
> The children, large and small,
> Whom we must save,
Turn their eyes forward to the land to learn.

Those children's hopes are here aboard with me,
        Adrift, adream, at sea,
    The peaks of home receding,
Alert for land across the wrinkled moat
Of ocean, without confidence or pity,
    While the strangely guided boat,
        Nobody heeding,
Moves its unknowing cargo toward the city.

Love, though I left you, smile on my return
        From the ancestral shrine
    Where blood will not again be spilled.
I would not travel now except to learn
More than the city teaches about sin:
    First, that that blood must be fulfilled;
        Second, that it is mine;
Third, that the island cannot take me in.

    Halfway between the city and the island I
        Am bound for the city.

4. *The Immigrant's Apology*

You think me citified, love?
Hard-shelled, headstrong,
Undoing all errors
With deftly trained fingers?

I am forced to step shrewdly
Through these byways perilous.
From every casement lewdly
Leans a crowd of faces of girls.

I am an islander, love,
Trained in taboos (Never touch
Hate with your left hand!),
Nourished on little and much,

Bred to believe
That ghosts guide bodies.
City ghosts do not bleed
With this our blood.

The journey here was long,
The boat, small,
Contrary winds, strong.
The sight of the towers was fearful.

Over the black pavement
Insect natives carry
Skeletons outside their flesh;
They click, they scurry.

My bones, love, lie in hiding.

5. *Travelling Among Islands*

(for Alastair Reid)

Alone, alone but not without resources
Even in his melancholy smile,
He keeps as property no more than a razor
And a laundered shirt to take him through tomorrow.
Clean as a cat he sits, nibbling his fingers
To make himself still cleaner, tooth and nail.

Love he knows in plenty—all the love
A sailor finds in port, with every girl flowery—
But he loves them dearly as they wave goodbye,
And all his friendships are perfect in chance meetings.
Departing, he leaves others to remember
And moves toward another destination
Where faces will wash clean again to see him.

Only the sea is home to him.
He is nourished by land as others are by water.
He lives on less than would supply a lifeboat
And his lovers lie in wait among the islands—
Circe, Penelope, Nausicaa, Calypso.

DANCE OF THE SHAKING SHEETS

Once we have discovered
How the heart grows old,
Leaving us no house
Against the cold,
We huddle for survival
And enlace
Body into body,
Face to face.

Hungry for compliance
That we once possessed
In the days of lap,
The days of breast,
We curl in the nest
Where we lately lay,
Savoring its softness
One more day.

There we know no hunger.
Surely more alive
Than when awake,
We shall survive
Stuttering rifles,
Deaf to the spit
Of angry bullets.
Let them hit.

Muffled under cover
We can bear
Any victim dying
Anywhere.
Rocking in the cradle
Of a lover's thighs
Softens the hunger
In her eyes.

Danger cannot penetrate
This womb.
Body, give us shelter.
Banish doom
Distant as the rifles
In the war
We refuse to study
Any more.

RITES OF PASSAGE: 1946

Through a window the wind
Went leafing through my book
A chapter at a time.
A fearsome way to spend
Those Saturdays in June—
Stealing my hundredth look
Past the ice cream saloon
While studious prose and rhyme
Stood sentry to my crime.
The summer dusk inex-
Orably drew me where
The tyrants of my sex
Should stand and smoke and stare,
Shuffling outsize feet
At the corner of our street.
This summer was the first
That brought me to that town.
Our house was tense and small.
Those boys were large and brown.
No matter what the thirst
That drove me to the shop
Where they had gathered first,
I trembled lest their call
Might summon me to stop.
They whistled at the skirts
And laughed with hideous
Suggestion at a blush,
Still louder at a glance,
And felt their khaki pants.
They combed their oily mat
Of hair. They yawned and spat.
Their names I had not learned,
But others of like size
Had bullied me at school,
Connived with me in lies,
Had hurled and batted balls
With brilliance and surprise
And trained me in the rule

Of locker rooms and halls
Where victory was earned
And secret passion burned.
What was there to know?
The thunder that we heard,
That turned us limp and pale,
Our clumsy bones absurd,
Our fingers aching from
The need to touch and tell
The belly's muscled swell
That one was not enough
To sample smooth and rough,
To hold heat in the palm—
Ah, what was there to know?
Inveigling with a hand
At night, by day we spoke
In arrogance and brags,
In excrement and leer
And hunted down the weak
Like poisoned contraband.
The weak were always fags.
The strong were never queer.
Give me another smoke.
Look at these knockers here!
The girls we left behind
Lived in another age,
Walked gracefully as foam,
Looked down, were soft and still,
Giggled when put out
For lack of fist or shout.
They could not have been real.
No wrestling? No rage?
No laughter? Who can win
When there are only smiles?

Here in a strange town
I stand before a book
In a climate swollen with men
Who scuffle and leer outside

Across a street I cannot
Cross, a lifetime wide.
For nearly twenty years
I shall not turn again
To hang around with the boys,
To lean and take a look,
To whistle at my fears.
I shall burrow among women.

LIFE MASK

The self inscribes itself upon the face
With signs that age alone cannot complete
Before the mask has settled into place.

Appetite, sorrow, labor, all compete
For every pore of skin and ridge of meat.
The self inscribes itself upon the face.

Beauty fell back, already in retreat
Before the heart sat steady in its seat,
Before the mask could settle into place.

My face, a stranger in the mirror's neat
And family frame, had many friends to greet.
The self inscribes itself upon the face.

Deface, defy, distract, corrupt, or cheat,
Whatever the name, the face will show defeat
Before the mask has settled into place.

My paces not yet learned, I set my pace.
By forty, someone said, the tale's complete.
The self inscribes itself upon the face
Before the mask can settle into place.

LUNCH AT THE COQ D'OR

The place is called the Golden Cock. Napkins
Stand up like trumpets under every chin.
Each noon at table tycoons crow
And flap their wings around each other's shoulders.
Crumbling bread, I sip at the edge of whisky
Waiting for my man to embody himself
Until in time he shadows the head waiter
And plumps his bottom in the other chair.
Once he is seated with his alibis
We order drinks, we talk. His voice is rich.
Letters I had written him all winter
Had washed my mind of him, till Purdy,
Warm of heart and hearty of handshake,
Had shrunk into a signature, a stamp.
The fine print vanishes. I see him plain.
I know my man. Purdy's a hard-nosed man.
Another round for us. It's good to work
With such a man. 'Purdy,' I hear myself,
'It's good to work with you.' I raise
My arm, feathery in the dim light, and extend
Until the end of it brushes his padded shoulder.
'Purdy, how are you? How you doodle do?'

THE FIRE IN THE HOUSE

O what a fire! It keeps me simmering
Without a thought a week of cinders
On fuel aimlessly procured by windfall:
Contradictions, insults and offenses
Trivial enough to catch a glow
Even when the branches are too green to snap.
All day they burn, not breaking into blaze,
But smolder, scarcely eagerer
Than rust collecting on a castoff pickaxe.
Yet under these pliant ribs
There's always fire enough
At a gust from the right direction
To bellow instantly into forge-hot flame
For tempering razors, smelting a world of ore,
Or burning the very house that harbors it.

THEY THAT HAVE POWER TO HURT

Hand me the knife. There. See?
It has no harm in it.
The blade is merely steel,
Slightly chilly, as if
Shrinking away from itself.
The handle, comfortable
To any hand, can rest
In yours as well as mine.

Now feel the natural
Sag of your fingers, with
This guest aboard. Mankind
Was never itself until
It learned to take tools to task.
Knife is the tool of tools.
Who can play the man
Without regard for weapons?

Now the next step. Slicing,
Chopping, scooping
Are among the ways of women.
With this male friend to hand
Consider alternatives:
The sweep, the stab, the slash,
The parry, drawing lines
With a well-inked brush
In the pure color of blood;
And conclude: the tugging gesture
Of withdrawal and extrication.

These are only the first
Of lessons in harm's way.
Knives are a source of light
To explore the paths of the body.
Find a space for the edge
And your blade will never be blunted
But may probe and search the flesh
For the live parts, or even the dead,

To let the living out
For everyone to see.

The final lesson is this:
The man who holds the knife
Contains no more keenness
Than what he grasps.
Nor is the knife the ruler.
Your knife is neither tool
Nor weapon, neither a means
Nor an end. The knife is you.

MAGPIE

Eight-toes, teetering
    Sabre unscabbarded,
        Bellying spinnaker

Fast to a fencepost,
    Gape your black bill
        In a squawk clean as kindling!

On, with a smother
    Of saw-toothed wingbeats,
        My piebald jolly-boat!

Surge hull down
    Past the crest of the ridge
        Where the wind breaks, breaks
        All day like foam.

EURYDICE IN DARKNESS

Here far underground I can hear the trees
Still moving overhead where he, the poet,
Mourns. Let him stir stumps if he chooses.
Soon enough he'll sing his courage up
To penetrate the earth, clinging to that lyre
As though the world depended on it, and unstring
One after the other of my familiars,
(The three-headed lapdog, the boatman at the river,
The gaggle of furies, my Undertaker himself)
With instrument still twangling from the effort.
His fingers will be raw, but I'll be waiting
Dressed to kill and ready with a plan
He'll find acceptable. He'll turn his back
(Its every flabby muscle I have pinched
A thousand times) and clump along the tunnel,
Dead certain I shall follow him to sunlight.
And so I shall—murmuring at times,
Whining that he walks too fast, complaining
That he might at least give me a look
After such absence, brushing my breasts against him.
Not till the sunlight seeps in overhead
Will I tax him: a man and not a poet
Would have kept the country free of snakes
And left off that everlasting mooning and fiddling.
He could have prevented all this! And he might, please,
Give me a hand here, I'll fall with these sandals.
That's it! He turns from the light, his face engorged
With pity and self-pity. He thrusts out his hand,
And I shall dance away, my laughter dancing
Before me every mile of the way back home.

HAVING SAINTS

God has become too vast to pray to
for anything in particular. Not so saints.
Saints have at least a mouth to be remembered.
They did not build the world. They carried
only their own burdens. God is beyond us,
inhumanized by the long passage of time
since anybody saw Him. Even His mother
has stiffened over the centuries, until
the Church, recently, promoted her into heaven.
Saints have their presences on earth, thank God.
They carry keys or swords, they visit prisons
or in unhappy times have their breasts torn off
by pincers, even as you and I.
We're not ashamed to tell our small desires
to Paul or John or Nicholas or Teresa
in hope they needn't be passed on through channels.
We may even confess to them our grudges and panics.
A saint can be bargained with, done honor to
in exchange for favors granted, can be asked
to set his kindly parasol between
the searing sun and my poor eggshell head.
Prayers and pleading lie not so far apart
to give all praise to God, no plea for myself.
No god worth worshipping would listen to
a prayer that had no sources in desire;
but One who spins the galaxies is not
an Ear to whisper into. Lord, give us saints
even if we elect them for ourselves.

EASTER ISLAND: THE STATUES SPEAK

We are asleep, at peace. The grass has woven
A blanket for the fallen few who lie
Dreaming supine, watching the trade-wind clouds
Glide overhead. Our uplands are deserted.
Safe in settlements along the sea,
Shepherds avoid the hillsides we inhabit.

Now come newcomers, bringing means to force us
To rear up again, hillbound on rocky haunches,
Pitilessly to search the sea-surface
And guard the grassblades in their little seasons.
Aboard new rafts that snuffle past the reef
They make for landings on our lava beaches
To set about their plan for resurrection.
They hope by disinterring us to save
Themselves from meeting themselves at the fatal crossroads.

Our feet stood fathoms underground. Thin soil
Clothed us to our chins. How we hoped
To be forgotten! Now these new arrivals,
Who place unearthly burdens on God, unearth us.
They prop us upright for the hundredth time.
They will gladly let us sleep again
Once they have learned the reasons for our silence.

FROM

THE BREAKING OF THE DAY AND OTHER POEMS

(1964)

And Jacob was left alone; and there wrestled
a man with him until the breaking of the day.
GENESIS 32:24–30

FOGGED IN

All afternoon the bank
Had pressed on sullenly
Up channel. Quick east winds
Butted against its flank.

It drooped beneath the blue
Like rags hung out to dry.
Sun seared its top, while sea
Supplied it from below.

Yet nightfall in its turn
Gained ground upon the sun.
This morning, under shield
Of darkness, fog has won

And blurs us deaf and blind.
Enshrouded beyond call
We tremble for the end
Of islands, echoes, all.

"TRUE FEELING LEAVES NO MEMORY"

The havoc of your gaze is tidy now;
The slow heat of your shoulder cooled long since.
Yet once the air bristled at the approach
Of so much as your finger to my elbow.
Memory leaves me no more than a flash
Of full moon glinting on unfrozen river.

Along the rolling pathway of my time
I can number the grassblades and forget-me-nots,
Though whole meadows are missing from the calendar.
I touch my finger to distorted roots
And track their features to a severed stump
That stops itself far short of boughs of zero.
What woodsman crept up with his silent saw
To cut this alteration on my landscape?
He finished off with cold purgative fire
To eat the tender wood, the loving leaves
That whispered once against themselves like thighs.

Returning now, I walk through open reaches
Naked to all, where I must once have lain
As warm as a rabbit's beating heart
In a thicket sprinkled with morning, where each leaf
Burned green, hot as a newly-minted coin.

NORTH SHORE

(For Charles Hopkinson)

1. *The Embarkation for Cytherea*

The sun is high. Young Saxons shouldering oars
Trample the shaven lawn. Platoons of girls
In organdied profusion follow them,
Flowers of Boston's bright virginity,
Cool limbs beneath frail garments. At the pier,
Piled high with picnic baskets, cutters ride
The hospitable swell, their halyards eased
Yet eager to spread sail. Across the strait
The islands rise like rain-clouds from the sea.
Here on our hill the house, after its crowded morning,
Will sleep till dusk. Then we expect them home,
Their wine all drunk, their faces gorged with sun,
Guiding their ships, with briny headsails furled,
To quiet moorings.

2. *The Return*

                    Many years have passed.
The house and I still wait for their return.
Shutters keep out the sun, chairs lie in shrouds,
The Chinese vases rattle with dry leaves.
Angry with age, but waiting, I keep watch
High in the eastern wing, my spyglass cocked
To sight the flicker of those homeward sails.
Perhaps they are all dead? I have not heard
A youthful voice for years. When will they come?
The sea still glimmers, empty of islands now.
The lawns are empty. Over the weathered house
Gulls hover, wailing their disdainful cry.
At night the house is silent, and the wind
Steals out each dawn to comb a barren sea.

WINTER SUNRISE

The crooked shall be made straight, and the rough places plain ...

Our valley's liquid throat is choked;
Its birches bow, their music halted.
Every valley has been exalted
Under this morning's lavish gift.
Yesterday's whirling storm invoked
Great calm. The snowy land is cloaked
In sunlight for a sacrifice.
The wind has lost its strength to lift
A single crystal from the drift.
The crooked straightens. Harsh hills
Crouch down beneath a roof of ice.

Every valley has been exalted,
Yet winter knows no sure device
To keep rough places in subjection:
With the shrug of a wing a blue jay spills
An avalanche, and lawless wills
Fall out of patience with perfection.

AT THE SITE OF LAST NIGHT'S FIRE

I scrape char off a board with a dull knife.
Unravelled into dust, black yields to gray,
And eager wood emerges from its mask.
Once it is stripped, the wood glows naked as bone,
Charged with light, suited to hands again.

To comfort this unstrung household, tiles of carbon
Clothed the sweet pine in velvet, muffled all
The liveliness that leaped within the wood
Through post and beam. Is it a fact that fire
Yesterday prowled up the stairs, munched at a floor,
Crumpled a roof, and tempted four upright walls
To tilt themselves into this last embrace?

Within my clothes I shiver at the scars
That overgrow delight and heal away
The marks where bumbling flame has licked my face.

NOT FORGOTTEN

(In memory of N.W.D.)

1. *Watching Her Go*

Drawn by her mumbled entreaties,
We gathered wordlessly around her bed.
She lolled there, shrunken, grizzled,
Garlanded in feeding-tubes, damp with sweat,
Plucking, when she remembered,
At the dressings from the last operation.
Look! Could she have stirred at the touch
Of my hand? Or was it another wave breaking?
The eyes opened. Pain burst at me
As from a cannon's muzzle.
They closed. Flaccid, fumbling
At the unravelled edge of herself,
She died like an otter sliding into a pond.

2. *Dream*

I stood alone at a funeral. It was up to me
To pronounce the oration. My tongue was knotted fast,
And every mourner rolled his maggot eyes.
The reek of greenhouse flowers pressed on ears
Still filled with Handel's "Largo," while the bright box
Gleamed like a conference table proof against speeches.
Toward the rear of the chapel, twisting kleenex,
Sat ranks of visitors, urged to stop in on their way
To another appointment by friends who had assured them
This would not take long. It was taking longer and longer.

Who was dead? It was up to me to remember.
I had ransacked my pockets twice—no memoranda—
And my Oxford Book of Consolations had vanished.
The penguin crowd creaked folding chairs impatiently.
So with nothing at all to say, I did what I did:
Danced a very respectful dance on the coffin.
The guest of honor drummed her cold toes
On the underside of the lid.

3. *Reality*

Have I no right to howl—not even now
When the cradle has been empty and cold for years,
The feeding-bottles broken, the rocking-horse rusted,
The christening-spoon bequeathed to hungrier mouths?
Her friends owned her as well: she had nursed so many.
They came together at last, a crowd collected
To watch the last flutter of a fountain, and turned away
As workmen tramped in to pry up the ancient stones.
But they turn away with a sigh: they cannot howl
Simply because they are not frightened enough.
They have lost a landmark, not a birthplace.

4. *Self-Defense*

I came to hold her hand
And sit beside her bed.
Her body was lightly manned:
The siege was in her head.

She counted rags of rage
And wore them while her breath
Grew shallow stage by stage;
Yet persevered in wrath

Against the runaway
Who roused a million cells
To take to their dying day
The habits of cannibals.

Her courage conquered me.
When she asked an end
I yearned to grant her plea,
To serve her like a friend.

Now I can weep no more.
My pain is almost mute.
I did not lock the door.
I did not execute.

175

5. *Aftermath*

The world now has
A gray look to it.
There is much less strangeness
Left in strangers.
Mountains have shrunk,
Trees loom with less shadow,
Even the flavor of fear
Tastes as diluted.

Yet the bloom of your presence
Is absurd as unicorns
Or buttercups at Christmas.
Just as your girlishness
Glanced out daily
From within thickened
Middle-aged flesh,
So does memory
Find you hovering
In a hundred places
Or standing
At the center of the music.

I pray you, do not stray
Farther from us.

DEATH SONG: THE MOMENT

The summer day is kind. A breeze
Surrounds me, as if tenderness
Were its invention. Set at ease
With all my selves, I smile and bless
    These friends: the leathern sage, the mild
    And unambitious aging man,
    The rebel boy, the gifted child.

I bring no trophies from the past
And wish for none. The Deathless Four
I was when young have merged at last.
Time was I wanted nothing more.
    Reduced to one, a single breath,
    The weather breathes me in and out
    Till I shall join with it in death.

Bordered by forest palisade
Whose stiffened hemlocks creak and groan,
A clearing keeps me in its shade
Until I come into my own.
    The waxwing grass has just the hue
    Of glossy hair I loved the most.
    That truth, at least, was not untrue.

I gave away what self I had
To love and loyalty. No doubt
What use they made of it was mad,
But could not self be done without?
    The breezes curry me as though
    Their mind turned on a single breath
    To keep me or to let me go.

The sky is higher now. The sun
Has dwindled to a coin of gold.
I cannot hear the river run.
The forest shade has lost its cold.
    The weather takes my breath away.
    This is the place prepared for me
    Where, without menace or decay,
    The earth will set my body free.

LATE SUMMER LOVE SONG

The evening's first cricket
Shrank from your passage
As your feet whispered
Past where he pastured.

Now the sun steals
A last look through the orchard
Where you lie low,
Fragrant in meadow.

Hear my blood welcome you,
Giddy with gratitude
For what shall pass
In the intricate grass.

SUMMER SCHOOL

These tenants of the migratory season
Were children yesterday. Adulterers today,
They settle like thievish cuckoos in such nests
As they can find furnished with a summer vacancy,
And share their sandalled quest of the absolute.

Professor P., expert in semantics,
Teases their drowsy mornings with a lecture;
But once the sun announces afternoon
They strip naked in each laboratory sublet
Among worn counterpanes and last winter's books
To dedicate each fiber of themselves
To the hot discipline of appetite.

Thus in the academy of summer
These scholars, sworn to seek the limits of self,
Enlarge their own by feeding upon others
And learn by process of elimination.
What bones will they have gnawed when they return
To the major business of the autumn
With knitted brows, to read once more of love?

THE PEEPER

No sound—yet my room fills up with thunder.
Behind their windows ladies dance for me,
Heedlessly languid, moist, sumptuous,
Naked as newts. Oh with what zest
Have I applauded wifely treachery,
Lovers in closets, husbands unsuspecting,
Greedy embraces once the door has shut!
Lit by electric light, flesh in a window-frame
Gives pleasure keener than clasping lovers know,
And I make no objection if the shade
Snuffs out the final postures of the act.
Night is my library; day deafens me.
I cringe to hear girls gossip, clatter round corners,
Scold shabby neighbors, squeal at the bus to stop.
Flesh under glass strikes no such dissonance,
Nor troubles touch nor smell nor taste. Away!
    I love at eyes' length!

PERIPHERAL VISION

The corner of the eye
Is where my visions lie.
A startle, or a slant
From squirrel, bird or plant,
Turns hard and fast if seen
By eyes asquint and keen.

Rather the shape and style
That only just beguile
The tail-end of my sight
Than organizing light
To tidy up the view
And clear it out of true.

THE FIRSTLING

Down the soft hillside
The farm girl came frolicking,
Rosy and ribald and
Looking for company.

Quick by a willow she
Stripped for the cooling brook.
Over her bursting breasts
Water meandered.

Soon she lolled ripe for the
Fumble of fingers, the
Plunging of pulses, the
Lovely unstringing,

But shortly, unhandled, she
Mounts up the hill again,
Carrying news
To set loose in the village.

How many summers had
Man and boy come to strive
With the nymph naked,
And all been rewarded—

All but this firstling, who,
Shirking his trial, lies
Dry-mouthed and still
Beneath the charmed hill?

SACRIFICIAL MASK

Mirror, Mirror on the wall,
Who is falsest of us all?

Only silence. Does this mask
Hear no questions mirrors ask?

I have modelled every crease
To ensure the people's peace

Who go easy when they see
Kindly love encasing me.

Now the eyes behind the face
Blink their horror and disgrace.

They know well what price was paid
For the features I have made.

THE STAR WATCHER

(For R. F.)

Stars had the look of dogs to him sometimes,
Sometimes of bears and more than once of flowers,
But stars were never strange to him because
Of where they stood. We knew him jealous
And in his younger days a little sly
About his place among the poesies;
Yet when his eyes showed envy or delight
They rested upon knowledge, not on distance.
All that he saw, up close or farther off,
Was capable of being understood,
Though not by him perhaps. He had enough
Of science in him to be optimistic,
Enough of tragedy to know the worst,
Enough of wit to keep on listening,
Or watching, when it came to stars. He knew,
Across the distance that their light might travel,
That nothing matters to the stars but matter,
Yet that their watchers have to learn the difference
Between the facts of knowledge and of love,
Or of love's opposite, which might be hate.
Therefore he taught, and, like the best of teachers,
Often annoyed the students at his feet,
Whether they learned too much or not enough,
Whether or not they understood him wrong.
Two was his pleasure, and the balance held
In love, in conversation, or in verse.
With knuckles like burled hemlock roots, his hands
Had, in his age, smooth palms as white as milk;
And, through the massy cloudbanks of his brows,
His eyes burned shrewdly as emerging stars.

TO A MAD FRIEND

I may look fine at the moment, but like you
I have capered and somersaulted in the street,
While, hoisted upon my shoulders, someone's face
Smiled at my friends and answered the telephone;
Or hovered, like a fish with nose against
A rock, in elements I could not breathe.
You've seen us in every land you've travelled through:
Our ties were tied, our shoes were always shined,
But icy eyes and tightness around the smile
Are marks enough to know your brothers by.
Rest easier, friend: we've all walked through your dreams
And are no strangers to that company.

FINALE: PRESTO

"I think I'm going to die," I tried to say.
My husband, standing over the bed, labored
To hear words in the sounds as they emerged.
He shook his head as briskly as a dog
Taking its first steps on land, and acted deaf
To the words he knew he might have heard me speak.
Throughout this evil month I've said the same
To every visitor. It comes out gibberish.
The night nurse, hiding in my room to smoke,
My daughter, prattling anxiously of clothes,
My son, weary from four hundred miles
Of travel every weekend—all escape
By smiling, talking, plumping up my pillows.
I wrack myself to utter any word;
They reply, "Dear, I cannot understand you."
If I could move this hand, this leg, I'd write
Or stamp a fury on the sterile floor.
I'd act the eagle. I, who winced at death
If the neighbor's second cousin passed at ninety,
Who bore an ounce of pain so awkwardly
It might have been a ton, who fed myself
With visions of good order in a future
Near enough to reach for—I am cumbered
With armlessness, with leglessness, with silence.
To say the word so anyone could hear it!
Death, do you hear me, death? The room is empty.
Only the one word now, hearers or no.
I batter at it with convulsive shouts
That resonate like lead. Again. And now—
Listen—it rings out like a miracle.
No one stands near. The corridor is dark.
"Death." I sing the lovely word again,
And footsteps start to chatter down the hall
Towards my bed. Smiling at every sound,
I see that no one can arrive in time,
And I, emptying like water from a jug,
Will be poured out before a hand can right me.
That word raised echoes of a halleluia.
Death, do you hear me singing in your key?

GOODBYE

A sailing cloud of pipe smoke wrecked itself
Against the wall. He watched its noiseless crash
And waited among the memories of the room
For the expected footstep on the stair.
Last meeting. What would be said he knew,
Had known for months. The words had turned to stone
And now were to be quarried, shaped, laid in place,
Wrenched from where they had rested all this time.
A rattle at the door downstairs, the sound
Of feet ascending, steps with a slump in them,
As though the climber's bones had turned to chalk.
Then for the hundredth time, the handle turned,
The door opened before her, she came in.
Her smile gleamed out as she took off her coat,
And his eyes drank deep, thirst even now unquenched
For hair as tawny as a winter hillside,
Eyes blue and vague, hands with a milkmaid's grip,
Legs strong for walking. Beneath her clothes he could
Remember breast and belly soft as fruit—
Yet slack for him. Fruit never gave itself
Less eagerly to a hungry mouth than she did.

"Well." With another smile she took her seat,
Shook out her hair, waited as usual.
Her cigarette filled silence till he spoke.
"You came . . . We had to talk . . . It's time . . . You know?"
"Yes," she said rapidly, "I guess it is."
He'd spoken it all before—the give and take
Of weary argument, nothing to win or lose—
But now, with a growing chill, he knew his mind
Because her true indifference had come through.
All he had wanted was to win a debate,
Persuade her against her will she wanted him,
Make her admit it even though she lied.
The silence fell like snowflakes, and the swirl
Grew thicker, stronger, deeper. In his head
A frightened hammering began. This wasn't the way

He had expected it to be at all!
She wasn't there; she simply was not interested.
No argument—she did not care to argue.
Yet she was kind, and in her kindness waited
Till he should let her go. He came and tried
To touch her, touch her with his hands, since words
Had lost their power with her. But her flesh
Was hearkening to something else. He felt
He could shriek at her, and still she would be deaf;
Could strike her, and her body feel no blow.

Yet she was crying, staring straight ahead.
He knew the tears were not for him. "All right,"
He said, "I'm sorry this is how it ends,
But there's no point going on," knowing that he
Had to pretend to take the final step
Although they both knew it was long since taken.

A kiss upon the cheek, as for an older brother,
And she was gone. Her steps went slowly down
One flight, then headlong down a second, like
A bird who finds the door of its cage left open.
The street door slammed behind her, and he heard
The sound of it for hours, it seemed, because
The clang of hammers started in his head
Again, and now he knew they would not stop.

ARTEMIS

See how this girl, trim,
Fragile as porcelain,
Poises within herself,
Standing apart with hounds.

Chaste in her garments, loins
Crisp as a boy's, her knees
Rigid as spear-shafts,
She stares down a victim,

Lowers her eyelids,
Lets the white linen fall,
Stretches, as unaware
Of the blood rising,

Curls like a kitten,
Unclenches her fingers,
While her demented eyes
Flutter in hiding.

Now, when the hunt is closed
Hard on the quarry,
Savage in chase at last,
"Die!" she screams, riding.

THE SUICIDE

Poor starling. Her cry was sharp enough to draw blood
As she braced her whistling head and squeezed her feet
Clamp upon her local chimney top
And glared as hard as the sky that looked her down.
Taut-muscled on the ground, she pecked and pecked
Whatever she scratched up, never sure
Which grains were food, which grains were only gravel.
Just so her loves, random as a vine.
Curse those who kept her food from her until
She'd learnt their tricks! Her hungry eyes became
Their sentinels, on watch for where the heart
Lurked, to have it out and peck peck peck—
And yet her beak most often fell on bone
Until the day she turned it on herself
And dizzyingly sang, within her throat
The sigh of the slain, the grunt of the executioner.

THE BREAKING OF THE DAY

(Genesis 32:24–30)

1. *The Birthright*

A half-and-half affair, I grew from the union
Of a buxom, vital, Titian-haired New Yorker
And the cockerel moodiness of a Tyneside orphan.
She, in the gabble of Upper-West-Side tea dances,
Looked feverish when her father, the cotton merchant,
Stumped off to synagogue to pray for his brothers' funerals.
Later, she chose not to explain to me the difference
Between the Talmud and the Pentateuch,
And I, unlearned in the ways of Shabbas and Seder,
Had to read them up later in the works of Wouk.
Not until I got to be thirteen
Did it cross my mind I might be half a Jew,
And not until an angry schoolmate told me:
I heard the malice rising in his voice.

To take a step backward, look once more at my father,
Who rarely saw a Jew till he was twenty.
Sweet-voiced, he was made much of by the Rector
As he raised his boy soprano at St. Simon's
And learned his Apostles' Creed and Catechism.
For him a Jewess was rich with secret knowledge
And raven-haired—he'd read Scott and Disraeli.
Jews, on the other hand, were money-lenders.

When the schoolboy told me of my being Jewish
I asked my parents, Was he telling truth?
My mother said that they had *meant* to tell me.
My father said it didn't really matter
Because I was Anglican by half.
The question I had asked was left unanswered,
And all the knowledge that I got for asking
Was learning that they had no wish to answer
And that my question led to other questions.

2. *The Wrestler*

Fastened by the skewer of despair in a hotel room,
Steeling under anger and lust, the leers of the sergeants,
Bound hand and foot on a tufted counterpane,
I lay in prison while the night air hardened.
God burst in at last with the cry of a prairie rooster,
And in the dawn my heart began again.
My limbs were kindled with a course of blood,
And I shot from my cell into the sunrise streets
To trudge for miles while I turned a new weight in my hands:
Cherished sin, to carry for my burden—
Mine for my charge, my signal, my evermore mark,
That a single touch had bestowed, and not of my choosing.

After sunrise came the shock of daylight:
To grapple with my sinfulness I must
Put God in words. The only words I knew
Were those that God had spoken in his books,
The books that England had prepared for Him.

3. *The Gift of Tongues*

God my father spoke in the calm of evening.
He spoke in iambs beating in the darkness.
His pipe glowed and its vapor blossomed upward.
The child at his feet drank in the heady honey
Of his voice, his presence, his attention
While the elm-leaves rustled their assent.
The words he spoke—from Oreb or from Sinai—
Were, had I known it, many times outworn
Except for those that burned as his alone:

> *I shall come back to die*
> *From a far place at last,*
> *After my life's carouse*
> *In the old bed to lie*
> *Remembering the past*
> *In this dark house.*

His voice wore all the costumes of our tongue,
And in the dark I trembled at the golden
Din of the past resounding in my ears.
These were the words that God had always spoken,
As, "This is my beloved Son, in whom
I am well pleased." The words belonged to him,
And now, as their custodian, he gave
His hoard to me at night beneath the trees.
I counted them for years before I learned
The spending of them; yet I did not know
That he had given them away for good
And that from that night forward he would walk
The earth like any natural man,
His powers incomplete, his magic gone.

4.   *The Salt Land*

After baptisms, confessions, confirmations,
Communions by the dozen, rites and choirs,
Cranmer's great book was absorbed into my bloodstream,
And all the words turned into words again.
The fish died while I stood before the Cross:
Christ's blood, they said, was infinitely precious,
But all I knew of it was that they said so.

Later still I watched my mother's mother
(She wept because she must outlive her daughter)
Being interred at a non-religious funeral
With a eulogy delivered by her doctor
At a Lexington Avenue mortician's chapel.
This was the end. The Jewesses were dead.
My female life-line was extinguished.

5. *The Dead Sea*

The womb that held me in its lake is dry,
The bounty parched and powdered. He that held
A weapon or a scepter or a cross
Has lost the good of his grasp and sits in silence,
Who took it on himself to shake the earth.
You, mother, rocked me bloodless in my cradle
And yearned to free me from my ancestors:
The womb of the Goddess denied she had been born.

So both were outcasts from their ancestry.
No offerings for them, no worshippers—
Except for me, who worshipped in myself
Crude copies of their skilled originals,
To find at last, on the baked earth of this shrine,
That I am no more Christian, no more Jew.

The afternoon is dark and not with rain.

6. *Delphi*

The crackle of parched grass bent by wind
Is the only music in the grove
Except the gush of the Pierian Spring.
Eagles are often seen, but through a glass
Their naked necks declare them to be vultures.
The place is sacred with a sanctity
Now faded, like a kerchief washed too often.
There lies the crevice where the priestesses
Hid in the crypt and drugged themselves and spoke
Until in later years the ruling powers
Bribed them to prophesy what was desired.
Till then the Greeks took pride in hopelessness
And, though they sometimes wrestled with their gods,
They never won a blessing or a name
But only knowledge.
                    I shall never know myself
Enough to know what things I half believe
And, half believing, only half deny.

Born in New York, PETER DAVISON was raised in Colorado, served, at sixteen, as a Page in the U. S. Senate, attended Harvard and Cambridge Universities, and became an editor in book publishing at twenty-two. Since 1956 he has edited books for the Atlantic Monthly Press. He is poetry editor for *The Atlantic*. He was married, until her death in 1981, to the writer Jane Davison, the mother of his two children. For many years he has divided his time between metropolitan Boston and a salt-marsh farm in Gloucester, Massachusetts. He won the Yale Series of Younger Poets Award (1963) and a literary award from the National Institute of Arts and Letters (1972). In addition to seven books of poetry he has written a "personal history," *Half Remembered* (1973). In 1984 he married the architect Joan Edelman Goody.